THE

post christian

MIND

THE
post christian
MIND

EXPOSING ITS
DESTRUCTIVE AGENDA

Harry Blamires

SERVANT PUBLICATIONS
ANN ARBOR, MICHIGAN

Vine Books is an imprint of Servant Publications especially designed to serve
evangelical Christians.

Servant Publications
P.O. Box 8617
Ann Arbor, Michigan 48107

99 00 01 02   10 9 8 7 6 5 4 3 2 1

Printed in the United States of America

ISBN 1-56955-142-2

LIBRARY OF CONGRESS CATALOGING-IN-PUBLICATION DATA

Blamires, Harry.
The post-Christian mind : exposing its destructive agenda / Harry Blamires.
    p.   cm.
ISBN 1-56955-142-1 (alk. paper)
1. Christianity and culture. 2. Christina life—Anglican authors.   I. Title.
BR115.C8B495   1999
239'.7—dc21   99-14076
                                                               CIP

Contents

Foreword

"Aslan is Tash. Tash is Aslan." More than once these words, unexplained, appear in *The Post-Christian Mind*, almost as a recurring motto. What do they mean?

They come from an episode in C.S. Lewis' final Narnia tale, *The Last Battle*, where Shift the Ape browbeats and bamboozles the beasts into equating Tash, the devilish deity who is one of Narnia's enemies, with Aslan, the Christlike lion whom the Narnians love. Says Shift: "Tash is only another name for Aslan.... Tash and Aslan are only two different names for you know who.... Get that into your heads, you stupid brutes. Tash is Aslan: Aslan is Tash." The name "Tashlan" is later invented to confirm the identity. But when Tash and Aslan appear, embodying ferocious cruelty and lordly love, respectively, it becomes plain that they are distinct—and as different as can be.

What Lewis' story reflects is his view of the attempts of the liberal theologians of his day to assimilate the world's religions and religiosities to each other. As in the twilight all cats are gray, so in the second half of the twentieth century—what Blamires terms the post-Christian era—many have thought all religions must be substantially the same, however different in their outward forms. The idea has been taken even further since Lewis' lifetime.

Harry Blamires uses this motto in his writing not to emphasize the dream of a transcendent unity of religions, but to underscore the threat posed by a secularist culture that is subjectivizing, relativizing, fragmenting, destabilizing, decategorizing, and decomposing processes, hurrying us down the road leading to total nihilism, where everything is everything and so is nothing.

Blamires is a Lewisian, and pays his readers the compliment of assuming we are Lewisians too. He is one of a number on whom C.S. Lewis' mantle fell in a real sense. Like Lewis, he is British, taught English literature at the university level, and is a traditional Anglican "mere Christian." Like Lewis, his teacher at Oxford and later his friend, he has written prolifically, from textbooks in his professional field to Christian fantasy novels and diagnostic apologies for mainstream faith. His constant concern as a literary discipler is to display and defend the Christian way of thinking in a non-Christian world. To that end he wrote his classic *The Christian Mind* and followed it up with *Recovering the Christian Mind*. Now he gives us *The Post-Christian Mind*. Of an earlier Blamires book a reviewer said: "It reads like the mature reflections of a very wise uncle...," and the same can be said of what we have here.

The *Post-Christian Mind* is true journalism in the G.K. Chesterton sense: shrewd reporting of what people around us think and do, with interactive comment offered on a basis of common humanity, common sense, and Christian insight. The examples are mostly British, as one would expect, but the masterful clarity and precision of the analysis offers wisdom for us all. Lewisians and Chestertonians, come hither! You are going to enjoy this book.

J.I. Packer

One

The Post-Christian Mind

There is no doubt that, as the twenty-first century approaches, Christendom faces formidable hostility, not the least in those developed Western countries once regarded as bulwarks of Christian civilization. Looking around us, we Christians cannot but be aware of how powerful and insidious is the assault on the faith we hold, the faith we have assumed to be the foundation of Western culture. Current secularist humanism—a mishmash of relativistic notions negating traditional values and absolutes—infects the intellectual air we breathe. There is a campaign to undermine all human acknowledgement of the transcendent, to whittle away all human respect for objective restraints on the individualistic self. The hold of this campaign on the media is such that the masses are being brainwashed as they read the press, listen to the radio or watch TV.

The intellectual forces of the Christian Church need to be mobilized in answer to a movement whose leaders are involved, knowingly or unknowingly, in nothing less than the decomposition of our civilization. It is time to submit the half-truths and sly insinuations of the new anti-Christian establishment to ruthless scrutiny. We need to analyze the machinery of discourse by which it operates and examine the

9

verbal currency which it exploits. If we do, we shall discover that the more deeply we dig through the slogans and verbiage, the emptier the supposed foundations of the fashionable liberal relativism will be seen to be.

Earlier books of mine have pressed the need for maintaining logic and consistency in Christian attitudes to the world of action and the world of thought. They have defined doctrinal yardsticks by which those Christian attitudes can be clarified. The concept of a "Christian mind" proved to be a useful umbrella term under which to formulate the presuppositions undergirding genuinely Christian attitudes to the contemporary world and its culture. In defining specifically Christian attitudes, we inevitably uncover by contrast the preconceptions in contemporary popular thinking that are inimical to the Christian faith. Moreover, logic leads us willy-nilly to unearth evidence that current preconceptions basically antagonistic to the Christian faith infect the thinking of Christians themselves, not only at a popular level but also at the level of theological controversy.

In my previous ventures into this field the logical approach has been to make the Christian faith the starting point and to survey the contemporary scene in the light of its doctrinal formulations. My intention now is to start from the other side of the fence. We shall explore the kinds of views, attitudes and topics of discussion that fill the mental atmosphere around us, and try, thereby, to define crucial characteristics of current secularist thinking—in short, to grapple with the "post-Christian mind." The method will be to pinpoint the preconceptions undergirding popular contemporary attitudes and show how they represent positions antagonistic to the Christian faith.

For some decades we have had reason to wonder what would eventually happen to the popular mind as the traditional restraints of Christian culture were increasingly jettisoned, that is, as the remnants of belief in a supernatural order disappeared. After all, accepting a divinely granted human responsibility for one's course through time has long been a basis for upholding an ethic of self-control. Recognizing at least the possibility of judgment to come reinforced this ethic. Now the sad results of our loss are revealed. The popular mind has been transformed before our eyes. There is need for a systematic Christian analysis of what this amounts to.

Coming to grips with the post-Christian mind will not exercise the brain in the way it was exercised in defining the Christian mind. For there is no fixed body of opinion, no homogeneous set of principles, no philosophical rationale informing that amorphous accumulation of half-truths on which the popular mind is fed by the media today. It would be a mistake to look for system and coherence there. It would be like looking for signposts in a jungle. And that, as will emerge later in this book, is partly because the distinction between the Christian mind and the post-Christian mind is analogous to the distinction between civilization and the jungle, between order and anarchy. Whether a civilization is coterminous with the religious faith that informs it is a question which the experience of the twenty-first century may answer.

If we are to examine from the inside the machinery of contemporary error, we must step outside of our theological skins. Everything that gives shape and meaning to our conception of the span of human life derives from a system of beliefs that the post-Christian mind rejects. The Christian finds the ultimate meaning of things outside time, outside the boundaries of our earthly human career. For you and me, the Christian revelation makes sense of all history and of all our human experience. The great drama of Creation, the Fall, redemption and salvation is something which for us overarches all human experience, to give meaning to our days. We have been told after what model men and women were fashioned, what demands are made of them and how they will be called to account. We are taught that there should be no point at which the will of God and the divine scheme of salvation is not relevant to what we are doing. This should be the unifying factor in our lives, giving purpose and coherence where otherwise there would be only what is discrete and disconnected, haphazard sequences at the raw animal level.

For where can they turn in search of meaning, purpose and coherence, those for whom the facts of Christian revelation are nothing but an idle dream? Can we lay aside our theological presuppositions, throw off any sense of life's structured purposefulness under God and look out on experience as the pure secularist sees it? If we try, we shall find that things fall apart, the center cannot hold. There is fragmentation, nothing to provide a meaningful linkage between the diverse experiences of your life or my life, except that you or I partake as an individual in all of them. In other words, if no meaning can be found in the objective scheme of things, then it must be sought in the experiencing subject—in you or me, the individual.

Is it any wonder then that we are experiencing this drift of contemporary attitudes which tries to locate whatever principle of unity life may have in the person of the experiencing subject? If there is no divine plan, what other unifying principle can be discerned in things, what design, what overall purpose, what guidance for human conduct? Codes such as the Ten Commandments or Christ's Beatitudes assert an objective moral authority overriding all individual opinions or tastes. But the post-Christian mind rejects such objectivities. Having turned its back on all notions of the supernatural, the very basis of the Christian belief in a rational order, it can look for authentication of its judgments only in the individual self.

The post-Christian mental world is not a world of structures but a world of fluidity. What issues from the mind bereft of divine affiliation is passing opinion, transient feeling, today's or tomorrow's capricious preference. The universal language of reason and morality gives place to a wholly relativistic vocabulary of emotive predilections. The standard articulation of moral judgments in terms of virtues and vices gives place to a strange amalgam of subjectivist concepts, such as self-esteem and self-realization. We are always hearing that someone has found himself or herself, gotten to know himself or herself, learned to live with himself or herself. On all sides people are prating about discovering their "identity," as though one could help having one. A figure famous in the eyes of the media's public will explain, "I found out who I really am," after some remarkable experience and as a result of some mighty effort. Most of us acquire this knowledge before the nursery school age. Incidentally, the Christian call to lose oneself stands at the very opposite pole of experience to these meaningless assertions.

As we examine this and that piece of evidence, and see what kind of notions are at large among the bulk of our contemporaries, we detect modes of thinking that are rooted in the cultivation of the comfortable self as the unifying ideal. That seems to be what it all amounts to. And this drift in secular exploration of the self has itself unhinged many within the Christian Church. Added to it, the need for living harmoniously in society along with people of other faiths has encouraged a pluralism that saps confidence in the imperatives of the Christian revelation.

We may well ask ourselves the question: How have we gotten to this pass? The mental climate no doubt always changes from generation to generation, but the shift, for instance, in popular moral thinking during the last few decades is surely a remarkable development. It is perhaps historically unique in its thoroughness. The Christian consciousness has been bulldozed into acquiescence in a society ethically remodeled beyond all recognition. Certainly, Christians of today face a mental world that their grandparents, if they saw it, would surely regard as exemplifying rather sleazy fiction. Let us try to put our fingers on crucial aspects of this transformation.

In the nineteenth century the threat to Christianity in the West was, in some respects, a clear-cut one. The development of scientific thinking encouraged an assumption that gradually a full understanding of the origin of the world and its inhabitants would be reached. This understanding would be such that past reliance on so-called revealed truth, as exemplified by biblical narratives and religious tradition, would be rendered unnecessary. "Faith" came to be regarded as a kind of provisional, presuppositional footing in an as yet unexplored terrain. It was an inferior substitute for knowledge, a substitute that humanity needed only where knowledge was not yet available. Progress toward true knowledge was a matter of patiently observing by microscope and telescope, assembling evidence and establishing conclusions.

It is important to understand the secularist perspective of the day if one is going to challenge it from the Christian point of view. It is also important to understand the secularist perspective of the day because it always infiltrates the Church. Thus in the latter part of the nineteenth century and in the early twentieth century the mode of scientific thinking that focuses on what is physically observable infected the Church. What came to be called the "modernist" movement within the Church sought to bring Christian experience within the scope of scientific scrutiny. As a result, a new skepticism was brought to bear wherever the supernatural impinged on the Christian story. "Modernist" thinkers tried to discredit doctrines basic to Christian belief—the Trinity, the Incarnation, the Virgin Birth and the Resurrection—and to explain away biblical narratives involving the miraculous. Thus the Christian faith was emasculated by trendy theologians too ready to accommodate their beliefs to the intellectual fashions of the day. The impulse to desupernaturalize Christian history and Christian teaching took hold of some who had previously been worthy believers. Nevertheless the so-called modernist movement did not irreparably muddy the waters of faith.

There were always, of course, scholars who defended theological orthodoxy and who resisted current aberrations. And in England, by the middle of the century, the testimony of more widely influential thinkers and writers such as C.S. Lewis and Dorothy Sayers, T.S. Eliot and Charles Williams had enlivened a renewed orthodoxy. Following in the footsteps of G.K. Chesterton, Lewis set out to reason people into Christian belief. The Christian faith was presented as the only thing that made sense of life and of the world. There was no attempt by Lewis or by others of his kind to underplay the demands of faith, to minimize the need for personally abandoning the self into the hands of our Lord. Indeed, the personal testimony Lewis bore was as compelling as St. Augustine's. But at the same time he overpowered the intellect in arguing the sheer necessity and the sheer reasonableness of the course of conversion he recommended.

Gradually the fashion and the taste for reasoning faded. I can locate the point in time, around 1960, when I became personally aware of how the change was affecting the popular mind. As a teacher, I had always found students responsive when the matter in hand led to some open discussion of philosophical or religious positions. Some such topic had arisen with a group of mature students, many of them former officers who had been retired from the armed forces by a national cutback. Interesting views were being aired when one student suddenly said, forcefully and in a tone dismissive of the entire discussion, "But this is the Age of Aquarius." That was all. And the implication of the words soon became apparent. Reasoning about basic issues of life and death, of truth and falsehood, of goodness and evil, was no longer valid. There were no longer any intellectual landmarks or signposts by which such reasoning could be conducted. Absolutes were nonexistent. The fluidity of experience was irreducible to formulation in concept or premise.

There were, of course, current movements of thought in the world of academic philosophy, such as the theories of the logical positivists, which played their part in influencing people to query traditional modes of reasoning. Philosophy at the specialist academic level seemed to preoccupy itself with casting doubt on whether the linguistic machinery by which it had always operated had any valid connection with living experience. Whether such thinking had much direct influence on the wider public is questionable. But obviously it contributed to undermining confidence in those who used abstract concepts in reasoning about the questions on which philosophical and theological thinkers traditionally made their pronouncements.

The course of the argument here is directed toward clarifying a change in the intellectual environment, subtle in its influence but sweeping in its implications. To say that reasoning was totally discredited would be an exaggeration. Rather, it was that to connect reasoning with living experience just went out of fashion. At the popular level, at the level of the glossy magazine, contrasts began to be drawn between what the head says and what the heart feels about this or that: opting for the action recommended by the heart was made to seem more adventurous, more up-to-date, less stuffy and, above all, less rigid than taking advice from the head. I emphasize the words "less rigid." Where intellect and feeling were in conflict, where wisdom and whim collided, it became the smart thing to reject the intellect and wisdom because they belonged to a sphere of rules and regulations, of fixities and demarcations, while feeling and whim inhabited the ever-changing environment of the fluid, the environment of the Age of Aquarius.

The scientifically based challenge to Christianity infiltrated the Church in the first decades of the century, and so-called theologians tried to whittle away its supernatural affiliation and to bowdlerize its dogma. The Aquarian drift of popular thinking has now infiltrated the Church. It has led the clergy to an emphasis on the immediate which is neglectful of history and tradition. It has led to an emphasis on emotional togetherness in delight as opposed to controlled obeisance in worship. It has produced a generation of clergy who try to please rather than to instruct, to appeal to natural inclination rather than to the sense of duty.

One difficulty that faces us is the fact that, during the last half-century, certain key words have been taken over by secular humanists and given connotations twisted to conform to their program of destabilization. We may cite words such as "freedom," "value," "rights" and "discrimination." These words, and many others, have acquired connotations explicitly adapted to the secularist agenda for decomposing the social and intellectual frameworks on which Christian civilization has been built. No weapon is more necessary today to the Christian apologist than that of verbal sensitivity. The abuse of words plays a key role in the decomposition of our moral and intellectual stabilities. In view of this, the reader will not be surprised to find some chapters in this book built around misused words, such as "rights" and "values." And, quite apart from such specific attention to misused concepts, the abuse of language will occupy us at many points in our exploration. Indeed, one reason why we define what we are up against as the "post-Christian" mind and not the "anti-Christian" mind is that current secularist humanism feeds on the inheritance of the faith it has abandoned. There is much in anti-Christian propaganda today—its vocabulary and concepts—that is essentially parasitical on the Christian tradition.

The aim of this book is to define what we Christians are up against in the areas where the new relativism is most threatening. It will involve disentangling threads of distortion and falsehood from the daily output of propaganda emanating from the media. Such clarification is badly needed. We Christians are not yet organizing ourselves, either by word or deed, against the incursions into our world from the world of unbelief. To what extent such organization is now called for will be made evident as we explore the current scene.

Two

Rights

I f we examine how the word "rights" is used today we shall see that individualistic notions of the human role have deeply infected the post-Christian mind. No longer do we hear simply of the rights of man or the rights of woman, of human rights and civil rights. Demands are now made in the name of children's rights and animal rights, minority rights and prisoners' rights, gay rights and lesbian rights.

We must bring a little logic to bear on this issue. The expression "gay rights" shows how grossly the word "rights" has been abused. Special rights do not attach to being homosexual any more than they attach to having red hair or being left-handed. You might speak of a defendant's right to a fair trial when he is charged with murder, but it is not by virtue of his being a murderer that he has that right. On the contrary, he has the right to a fair trial because he may not be a murderer after all. An individual may justly be said to have rights as a citizen, but a gay man cannot claim any rights at all specifically by virtue of his being gay. He enjoys the usual rights of a free man, but no distinguishable rights as a gay man. Nor, in fact, does he really want such rights. He would be the first to admit that he does not want to be distinguished from others in any context specifically because he is gay. What he really wants is to meet with exactly the same treatment as his happily married neighbor. In other words, as a gay man he wants the fact of his homosexuality to be of no account, to be totally disregarded when such matters as applications for jobs are concerned.

The Bill of Rights, which settled the succession of the English crown in 1689 and whose provisions, where applicable, were embodied later in the American constitution, spelled out the liberties of the subject under a specific legal code. It was designed to put an end to religious persecution. That all subjects have the right to subscribe to whatever religious faith they choose is a principle of a just society. But to say that a person has the "right" of religious freedom does not tell you anything about the person. It tells you something about the legal code to which the person is subject.

There are, of course, "rights" that properly belong to individuals. I have a right to live in the house which I have purchased. This right, however, is better called an "entitlement." English law and general practice in England still speak of the "title" and the "title deeds" in respect to property ownership. Notions of proprietorship properly belong to this kind of right or entitlement. There would be a sense of outrage against injustice if a man's claim to live in his own house were questioned. Something emotively powerful is stirred within us when we hear of any challenge to a person's rights in this respect. It is regrettable that, when we transfer use of the word "rights" out of this proprietorial sphere into the sphere where "rights" testifies to nothing more than allowances conceded by the criminal law, we carry along the emotive baggage that accompanies the word.

Human "rights" will not play much of a part in the thought and talk of a Christian. Where there is tyranny in government or injustice in a legal system, the Christian ought to be as zealous as anyone in resisting official pressures. But the Christian will not go around sticking the label "rights" on every human demand to be free of discipline, obligation and moral imperative. The word "right" cannot but carry with it a connotation derived from the basic distinction between right and wrong. It is an emotive word, and usage of it has corrupted the post-Christian mind as overtones of virtue and righteousness have been allowed to whitewash claims to unfettered practice of vice.

There is another sphere in which we currently hear abuse of the words "right" and "rights." The abortion debate gives us phrases such as the "right to choose" and a "woman's rights over her own body." In each case there is a parallel distortion of language. Free will is divinely granted to us. We can choose between good and evil: we can choose to be righteous or to sin. But the Christian knows that to choose sin is to forfeit freedom. That is the first message of the story of Adam and Eve and their fall. Freedom, for the Christian, consists in choosing obedience. You are acting freely if you play the good Samaritan at the roadside, but you are acting in slavery to selfishness if you pass by on the other side. To preserve an unborn baby is an act of freedom. In many circumstances in which it happens, to kill an unborn baby is an act of slavery to selfishness. The "right to choose" can never, for the Christian, be the right to sin.

Now we are perfectly aware that those who are possessed by the post-Christian mentality will reject these statements outright. But this book is not being written in order to achieve an accommodation between the Christian mind and the post-Christian mind. On the contrary, it is being written with the precise aim of highlighting the tremendous gap that has opened between the mind of the secularist media and the mind of Christendom.

Thus we can assert with assurance that, philosophically speaking, a woman's "rights over her own body" are non-existent. I do not mean this only in a strictly Christian sense. I do not mean only that none of us can have "rights" over what is intended to be the temple of the Holy Spirit. I do not mean only that we Christians have surrendered any such "rights." (For that is what baptism is all about.) No, I mean also that "choice" in respect to our bodies is a peculiarly irrelevant concept. We do not choose to be born. We do not choose to be male or female. We do not—what a pity, you might say—choose our own body. We have to accept it as an endowment wholly given to us. Yes, we should keep it inviolable. And we should submit it to uses for which the Creator intended it. But as for "rights" over it, why, our authority over it is so weak that we cannot prevent it from aging and decaying.

Whatever we may say in theory, in practice we know well the limitations of our authority over our body. We cannot deny to the influenza germ or the fever virus the "right" of entry to it, the "authority" for a complete takeover of it. Indeed, we have to respond to the body's demands upon us with slavish promptness. When these demands become pressing and clamorous, we have to run off to the doctor and have the body's latest requirements of us spelled out in detail. And woe be to us if we fail to respond to the body's dictates.

The imperiousness of the body's demands upon us and the groveling servitude with which we answer them makes nonsense of claims to unqualified rights over it. Whose impulse am I obeying and what is the authority to which I respond when I break inconveniently into my work schedule to attend a medical appointment, when I ponder the doctor's diagnosis, when I receive the prescription he presents to me, when I rush off with it to the pharmacy, when I study and implicitly obey the instructions on the bottle or the pillbox: "Three tablets to be taken daily on an empty stomach," or "Two teaspoonfuls to be swallowed after every meal"?

It is true that, in a certain crude sense, I can direct the motions of my body, other things being equal. I can order my hand to propel the pen across the page. I can order my legs to propel me across the room. I can order my arms and hands to remove a dictionary from the shelf so that I can consult it. I can direct my fingers to find the right page and my eyes to follow line after line. But can we seriously apply the word "rights" to this kind of mechanical operation? You would not speak of a steering wheel's "rights" over your car's direction, or the tuning knob's "rights" over the radio station it selects.

Many great saints—St. Paul, for instance—have eventually declared their desire to escape servitude to the body which this life on earth prescribes. Many poets—Shelley and Keats, for instance—have seemed impatient with the human being's imprisonment in the fabric of flesh and blood. Such people would surely have thought that to speak of exercising "rights" over their bodies would be like prisoners speaking of "rights" over their dungeons.

Common sense can help us here. How can you talk of

exercising the ultimate authority of "choice" over this thing that you earnestly wish shorter or taller, thinner or plumper, better proportioned and better complexioned, more graceful and more attractive, less weary, less worn, less wrinkled? Surely the pretense to exercise such authority is absurd. And how can you talk of enjoying the rights of free choice over this machinery of involuntary ingurgitation and exhalation, unpredictable in its bursts of indigestion and constipation, its bouts of headache and toothache, its susceptibility to rheumatism and arthritis, asthma, heart attack, paralysis, cancer and the rest? The idea of exercising the rights of free choice over it is lunatic. You might as well claim "rights" over the weather.

The truth is that Christian thinking does not focus on human rights but on human duties. The connotation of the concept "right" points back to the individual. The connotation of the concept "duty" points outward from the individual to some authority claiming recognition. But, of course, if there is no overall authority transcending that of the civil power, then the concept "duty" cannot be brought into play except within the sphere of civic and legal obligations. That being so, it is interesting to observe how the concept of "duty" has all but disappeared from modern thinking. We prefer the concept of "responsibility," which puts us in charge of things, to the concept of "duty," which points to authority outside and above ourselves.

Indeed, human duty, in the personal moral sphere, is an essentially religious concept. Yet I have heard a sermon in which the congregation was told that to attend church merely out of a sense of duty was wrong, that they ought to come because they wanted to, indeed, because they enjoyed it. Such a denigration of duty as a motive is a grave and dangerous error. And it is particularly out of place when the services in question are such that no one with any literary or musical taste could possibly take pleasure in them.

I once saw in a newspaper two photographs of people worshiping. The one showed a handful of people kneeling in a village church. The other showed a packed mosque with rows and rows of the human hindquarters of bowing worshipers of every age. The two contrasting photographs come to my mind whenever I hear a minister introducing some new vulgarization of worship on the grounds that it will "attract the young." What attracts those packed rows of worshiping Muslims? Their behavior testifies to a strong sense of duty. The last thing it suggests is that the worshipers are thoroughly "enjoying" themselves. Indeed, emphasis on worship as a duty to God ought to be the priority for all of us. It should supersede any specious notions of "attracting" men and women to a place of worship as though it were a place of entertainment.

There is a much-neglected poem by the poet who is often considered to be the arch apostle of veneration for nature, William Wordsworth. He was thirty-seven years old when he first published it. It is called "Ode to Duty" and begins:

"Stern Daughter of the Voice of God! O Duty!" It is not long before Wordsworth is making a remarkable confession:

I, loving freedom and untried;
No sport of every random gust,
Yet being to myself a guide,
Too blindly have reposed my trust;

And oft, when in my heart was heard
Thy timely mandate, I deferred
The task, in smoother walks to stray;
But thee I now would serve more strictly, if I may.

So in midlife the poet pauses to examine himself, and he has to admit that, under cover of a love for freedom, he has too rashly and hastily accepted the guidance of personal inner impulse, shrugging off the call for obedience to divine authority. The final stanza reads:

To humbler functions, awful Power!
I call thee; I myself commend
Unto thy guidance from this hour;
Oh, let my weakness have an end!
Give unto me, made lowly wise,
The spirit of self-sacrifice;
The confidence of reason give;
And in the light of truth, thy Bondman let me live!

So the great prophet of the Romantic revolution, the seeming advocate of nature's authority over us, finds his highest calling as a bondman to duty, the offspring of God's voice. Even so we are all called to recognize our creaturely status as men and women made by God and called to his service. That recognition will naturally impel us to ask, "What do I owe in return?" rather than "What more can I claim?"; "What are my duties?" rather than "What are my rights?"

Three

The Family

We have begun to hear conservative politicians talk about the need to defend "the traditional two-parent family." The use of this expression indicates that a change in public thinking is now confirmed. My dictionary defines a "family" as "the group consisting of parents and their children." For many centuries this definition would have been accepted. Indeed, earlier in our own century the adequacy of the definition would not have been questioned. Numerous as were the war widows after the First World War, struggling to bring up their fatherless children, the expressions "one-parent family," "lone-parent family" and "single-parent family" did not come into general use. Those widowed mothers of the interwar years would have been the first to admit that their children were being deprived of the fullness of "family life" by the loss of their fathers. They regarded their situation as one of serious deprivation. They would have been offended to be told that their little community was not impaired as a "family" after its bereavement.

There is a linguistic issue here. The relevant question is, "What is the norm?" If you were talking to someone about Robert Louis Stevenson's novel *Treasure Island* you would not say, "One of the crew is the one-legged sailor, Long John

Silver, but the rest of the crew are traditional two-legged men." Tenderness toward the feelings of people who have suffered amputations does not yet require us to pretend that the two-legged human being is not so much a norm as a variant. Of course, if by some unfortunate quirk of nature, a significant proportion of human beings began to be born with only one leg, the situation might change. It might be necessary on many occasions to specify a "two-legged" person as such. Instead of first asking whether a new baby were a boy or a girl, it might become fashionable to ask about how many legs the new arrival possessed. An interesting question arises here. At what point in the gradual increase in one-legged babies would it become, not just necessary, but natural to call the other ones "two-legged"? In other words, at what point does the norm turn into a variant?

The question is asked because in various fields of thought the conversion of norms into variants is a means of destroying standards. There are other spheres of usage in which we shall see this process at work. The word "family" provides a case in point. If and when the proportion of one-parent families reaches the point at which it becomes necessary to use frequently the expression "two-parent family" in order to distinguish the one kind of grouping from another, then the concept "family," as defined in my dictionary, will have disappeared. The "group consisting of parents and their children" will no longer be the norm. Instead the "family" will become "any grouping of parent(s) and their (his/her) child(ren)." One variant will be the single-parent family; another variant will be the two-parent family; and further variants will be the nonparent(s), male or female, plus nonoffspring amalgamations of different generations.

The verbal changes we have seen in this respect are not just accidental products of natural development. There are those in our society who are hellbent on destroying "norms" and relativizing standards. That is what is happening in the moral and social spheres. In areas of life dominated by material considerations a different situation obtains. Consider the world of dress, which is dominated by commerce through advertising. In that world norms are tyrannically imposed on the masses. In that world prescriptions lay down what the human body must wear with a dictatorial decisiveness that is cringingly obeyed. Whole generations can thus be brainwashed by commercial interests into wearing denim jeans as though they represented a high point of culture in terms of aesthetic appearance and practical convenience. These fashions are adopted by whole generations who pride themselves on their freedom from conventional inhibitions. We witness the spectacle of supposedly rebellious spirits kicking against convention while they are all garbed in the same uniform.

Meanwhile, in areas of life where norms might be more sensibly adhered to, they are resented because they make incursions into the sphere of the relativistic which the contemporary secularist mind increasingly inhabits. It is no accident that in the last few decades the word "stereotype" has become a pejorative term. The word is a figurative expression derived from the printing concept relating to a metal plate of typeset from which numerous identical copies can be made. Hence it is used of something continued or constantly repeated without change. But, except where commerce dictates otherwise, the post-Christian mind has an obsessive attachment to change and variation. Numerical preponderance of this or that "norm" is regarded as a challenge. Our case in point, the formerly accepted stereotypical notion of the "family" must be replaced by a more fluid concept that will embrace all kinds of variations.

In the same way the post-Christian mind tends to reject concepts that can be said to be in any way "exclusive." It will not have frameworks established which confine and restrict. Frameworks such as those of the traditional family are to be rejected and torn apart, because if you put a frame around anything at all, then there is something inside the frame and something left outside it, something included and something else excluded. This will not do for the modern liberal post-Christian mind for whom the pursuit of omni-inclusiveness must be presented as somehow virtuous.

The process of destroying standards relies heavily on the tendentious use of words. We do not find many people openly declaring war on "the family." The method of attack is to keep and use the word "family" but destroy its meaning. By this means the standards which usage of the word has previously sustained are obliterated. That is why the enemy of the true family does not usually condemn "the family" in so many words. Instead new terms are brought into use. We hear criticism of the "nuclear family" or the "traditional family." The propaganda advantage in popularizing such expressions is obvious. "Family" is a word which, over the centuries, has acquired warm, humane associations. Idealized pictures of conventional family groupings survive in art, in literature and in popular memory. The word "family" is likely to arouse emotive associations of homeliness, affection and warmth. The technique employed by contemporary decomposers of standards is to take over the traditional concept and deny its traditional exclusiveness—the thing that makes it what it is. Instead of attacking the "family" as such, they turn what we have always known as the "family" into a variant among other variants. In fact, the nonfamily (the very thing that the concept "family" exists to exclude) becomes a "family" too—perhaps two lesbians who are bringing up a child conceived in a test tube. Once the verbal process starts—of qualifying the norm, of speaking of the "traditional" or "two-parent" family—the game is lost. The assumption has been accepted that there are other kinds of families too.

The battle for morality and reason is often lost or won when a new verbal usage is accepted or rejected. We hear talk of "one-parent families" or "single-parent families" and we fail to register openly the query that lurks at the back of our minds. In so doing, we connive in a great pretense. Let us see by analogy how the process works. Suppose I wanted to make shoplifting respectable. I would cease to use words like "theft" and "burglary." I would refer to the act of stealing a gold ring from a jeweler's shop as an act of purchase from which money has been withheld, shall we say an "uncompounded purchase"? If I then start to refer to the ordinary act of buying something and paying for it as a "compounded purchase," I shall have brought into relationship the act of buying and the act of stealing in such a way as to suggest the two acts are not totally different practices but variants of the same basic practice of going into a shop and obtaining something. Obviously the expression "uncompounded purchase" would lend an air of respectability to the act of theft. But that air of respectability would be closely related to acceptance of the expression "compounded purchase" for honest buying. The moralist would have to begin to clear the air by pointing out that "compounded purchase" is an unnecessary and tautologous expression, because to purchase something in a shop is to acquire it properly in exchange for payment. The moralist might add that expressions like "two-parent family" or "traditional family" are equally tautologous. After all, the system of human reproduction is such that every child has two parents.

Here we come to the crux of the matter—the relationship between those two parents. The civilized West faces the new millennium with an unresolved problem about the relations between the sexes within the family. At the beginning of our century it was assumed that the husband's role in life was that of the wage earner and the breadwinner, while the wife's role was that of housekeeper and main nurturer of the children when they came along. It is understandable that in the days before electric cookers and washers, central heating and vacuum cleaners, at a time when families were often larger than they now are, the wife had a full-time job of looking after the young and running the home. It was not considered a less dignified or worthwhile occupation than going outside the home to work. Indeed, in the interwar period people turned up their noses in sympathetic pity for married women who "had to go out to work." Officialdom corroborated this attitude. A female employee in the Civil Service had to leave her position if she got married. When the Second World War began and the shortage of male employees compelled a change of attitude, the female employee who got married had her status changed from that of a permanent to that of a temporary employee.

One must not imagine that the country's total female

workforce in the early decades of the century was therefore small. Large numbers of women were employed in domestic service. Large numbers were employed in the textile mills. There were female office workers and shop assistants in abundance. But the general pattern was to treat these occupations as proper for the yet unmarried or for the widowed. And, of course, the First World War left the country with plenty of widows and plenty of single women whose would-be husbands had been killed.

The crucial difference now, as we approach the end of the century, is that the norm of married life has ceased to be that of working husband and housebound wife. Wives go out to work. The feminist movement can claim as a victory the removal of the once-dominant career pattern for a girl, the pattern that began with lessons at school in domestic science and needlework, and reached its apogee at the altar rail and in the duties of housewife and mother.

But it is possible to doubt whether this transformation of a woman's lot has been in all respects as positive a matter as the feminists claim. We hear people speak as though the single-salaried household of the midcentury decades was more straitened financially than its opposite number today. But, in fact, the contrary is probably the case. As long as the single-salaried household was the norm, house prices had to be within reach of its resources. As the double-salaried family gradually became the norm, so house prices were duly increased to match the greater resources of the average house-buyer. It can be seriously argued, in the United Kingdom at any rate, that one of the main achievements of the women's movement has been registered in rocketing domestic property prices. This does not, of course, constitute an argument in principle against the aims of any of the women's movements. Rather it points to defects in our economic system. It could be more easily registered as an attack on the free capitalist market than on the feminist movement.

These thoughts come to my mind as I read in my daily paper the results of a magazine survey whose findings were gathered from five thousand women. The summary of the findings makes quite startling reading. Seventy-four percent of the women have a full- or part-time job, but only nineteen percent are interested in a career. Seventy-eight percent would like to give up work. Thirty percent would like to stay at home with their children all the time. Fifty-two percent of those with children and who need financial help would prefer to have part-time work only. Half of the women who were working said they also did most of the housework. Those interviewed talked a lot about stress and overwork, and almost as much about money worries.

We can draw only the most general conclusions from such reports. Magazine surveys are not likely to be conducted according to rules that would satisfy professional statisticians. But clearly it can be seen that the replacement of the traditional Victorian family pattern of the breadwinning husband and the homemaking wife has not produced a satisfactory alternative pattern. Working married women who also do most of the housework have a just reason to complain. We must also take into account that in the middle classes, working husbands are often spending longer hours in business than their predecessors of three or four decades ago. The result is that many such households can be happily managed only if child-care workers are employed to look after the young.

Now it would be absurd to label the Victorian family pattern as specifically and uniquely "Christian." But it would be equally absurd to pretend that a family pattern satisfactory to Christians has been established to succeed it. And only by the diminution of Christian principles could we have obtained the present situation—one in which children come home from school to empty homes, where mothers are no longer always there as guides and caregivers, as advisers or consolers, to share the daily ups and downs of young life in sympathy and understanding.

Yes, we had a pattern of relationships which the Christian could appreciate and recommend. But that pattern has been destroyed and it has not been replaced. This development is in keeping with the gradual post-Christian rejection of those structures and frameworks, social and ethical, that distinguish civilized life from the life of the jungle.

It will be argued that this is an issue of equality between the sexes, but equality of standing should never be equated with identity of function. We hear a great deal of talk about the need to get equality of treatment for men and women in the labor force. No one would question the principle that there should be equal pay for equal work. But the thoughtful observer is bound to question some of the generalizations made on the subject by feminist agitators.

I have just heard a feminist declaring on the radio that no woman would want to suffer dependence on a wage-earning husband these days. Unless we look at the present age with eyes totally blind to past generations, we are bound to allow that millions of women of high intelligence and indomitable spirit have been quite prepared to be dependent on their husbands for their living. In any case, what is the alternative for a woman who is financially dependent upon a husband she has freely chosen to run a household for? There is only one alternative, and that is to be financially dependent upon an employer who graciously accepted her supplication for work. Certainly, to be at the beck and call of an employer is not more dignified than running a home for a husband and children. The homemaker has all-around advantages in terms of personal freedom. There is no area of experience today in which people are more susceptible to self-deception than in this matter of what constitutes true dignity and freedom in the ordering of responsibilities between husband and wife. Some of the ironies were pointed out decades ago in an earlier phase of the women's movement, when G.K. Chesterton observed that thousands of women had declared, "We will not be dictated to," and promptly took jobs as shorthand typists.

Four

The Family Under Attack

The civilized society is distinguished from the savage and the barbaric by the organization of its physical structures and the ordering of its social and intellectual structures. We all know what it means to destroy the physical structures of our civilization. We see it whenever war damages cities, transport systems, power supplies and the like. However, the preservation from damage of mere material structures will not maintain a civilization if its social, moral and intellectual structures are destroyed. Obviously, a nation that has lost its language and consequently all possibility of communication could scarcely be saved from barbarism. Similarly, as Shakespeare has illustrated so forcefully in *King Lear,* when a kingdom's ruler who has proper authority abdicates and hands over the reins of government to those whose only claim is their greed for power, then the forces of anarchy and criminality take over.

It is clear that evil forces in our age are directed toward the decomposition of the civilized society of the Christian West. One of the crucial social structures of our civilization has been that of the monogamous family. We have seen already how much it is under threat. Within the lifespans of many of our contemporaries propaganda has eaten away at the notion that the monogamous family built on lifelong marriage is the norm.

I pick up the daily newspaper. Dominating the front page is a large photograph of a happy, smiling couple at their wedding. As I read the caption, however, I gather that the bride, a star of the film world, is just acquiring her third husband. Indeed, today when we see a photograph in the press of a star in the media world or the sports world getting married, the marriage is quite likely to be the second, third or fourth for one or both partners. As difficult as it may be for the educated mind to accept, these stars are supposed to be "role models" and, in fact, are often popularly admired.

Earlier in our century, before the divorce rate escalated, the press generally would have dealt very discreetly with the remarriage of divorcées. We might have seen large photographs of happy couples on their wedding days, but not of divorced couples on their third or fourth wedding days. Readers, however, have been brainwashed into accepting serial polygamy as the norm. That is the kind of campaign to which press moguls are committed. It is a campaign of decomposition, of deconstruction.

There was a time not very long ago when simple people had their notions of propriety molded by church and school, parents and grandparents. But they now derive their moral and intellectual nourishment from other sources. They would once have been bred to the assumption that marrying involved a lifelong commitment to their spouse. They are now induced to acquire from the press and the other media a taste for the amoral habits indulged by the spoiled creatures of stage, screen and pop music.

We have all listened to sermons which made a crucial distinction between influencing others by word and influencing them by deed. We have often been told that it is by our example rather than by our utterance that we shall be judged. Has there ever been a time in the Christian West when preachers found it desperately necessary to exhort people to cherish the monogamous state? Certainly there was no time in the first half of our own century when sermons or Sunday school lessons dwelled largely on the need to restrict oneself to one wife or one husband till death. It was not necessary to urge people to follow a practice which almost everyone else was adopting. The example of deeds made instruction by words unnecessary. Thus it was, in previous generations, unnecessary for elders to instruct the young in a matter so obvious as the preservation of monogamy.

A battle has been lost by default. No one preached lifelong monogamy explicitly in words. But the media of the West set about the task of preaching serial polygamy by example—by example of the famous, the successful, the idolized. Here, before the eyes of the admiring young boy, this or that pop star or sports star takes his third or fourth bride into the sphere of being happy ever after. And there, before the eyes of the impressionable young girl, the glamorous film star gazes into the eyes of her fifth bridegroom and announces she has found happiness at last.

The same technique is succeeding in destroying the Christian belief that the procreation of children should be within marriage. In the past, it had never been thought necessary to include in sermons, parental advice or any kind of educational instruction the exhortation to keep procreation within marriage. The recommendation came through experience. The arrival of a baby to an unmarried girl might have been accepted with quiet charity, but that charity was adopted to veil an act rather too disgraceful to be openly talked about. Similarly, I doubt whether much explicit instruction has been used—or even needed—in revolutionizing the public attitude toward the intentional begetting of illegitimate children. No such change in teaching has been necessary. The media has taken over. This or that distinguished businesswoman, a top executive, is featured in the press and photographed in all her dignity and even beauty. She speaks a few words of good advice to aspiring young ladies. And, by the way, in parentheses, without fuss, it is revealed that she is an unmarried mother of a child or two by a father or two.

Such revelations are now a regular feature of the press. The brilliant author of some best-selling fiction, the accomplished actress or the TV personality of the year is featured in all her charm and charisma. Her achievements are listed; her qualities are described in superlatives. Here, indeed, is someone for the young girl to emulate. And, between the lines almost, it is added that she is the unmarried mother of a child or two by a father or two. There would be no point in making a fuss about this fact. There would be no point in emphasizing it. Why? Because you only make a fuss about what is remarkable or exceptional. You only emphasize what is extraordinary or surprising. You do not draw particular attention to what is normal and expected. That is how a nation's morals are corrupted. That is how the structures of a civilization are destroyed. That is how it has happened. That is how the battle has been lost, courtesy of the press barons, and courtesy of the media moguls. Nobody has explicitly preached a new doctrine. Nobody has openly proclaimed that the principle of procreating children only in wedlock is a thing of the past. But the example of the successful single mother is featured as a model before the ambitious young girls of our day.

Is it possible that we may see a turn of the tide? I have just read an interesting paragraph in my daily newspaper.

Welfare reform in Britain must be driven by painful financial sanctions for single parents and the unemployed to have any lasting effect, an American sociologist says today. Charles Murray argues in a pamphlet from the Social Market Foundation, an independent think-tank, that the main aim of reform must be to change behaviour, not to cut bills. Lone parenthood must be discouraged because it has strongly negative effects on children.

So, in the year 1998, we have discovered that lone parenthood must be discouraged because of the deleterious effect it has on children. Who will convey this message to those glamorous stars, those high-flying business executives, those ladies who charm us with their personalities in the media?

One of the difficulties facing Christians in this respect is that insistence on marital fidelity and the preservation of families can easily be made to seem priggish and excessively judgmental. So often great suffering is involved in the break-up of marriages. As a result, any word or attitude that is not brimful of compassion for unfortunate divorcés and divorcées seems out of place. And in consequence of this, Christians frequently find themselves caught up in sympathy with attitudes which their better judgment tells them should be queried. Moreover, because of this dilemma, it is all too easy for us to indulge, or even display, a tacit acceptance of behavior which, in fact, we really deplore.

We can illustrate the dilemma only by recounting records of grievous suffering which one hesitates to reproduce. It might be hurtful to people involved were I to cite in detail specific instances of the way our feelings can be worked on against our better judgment. I shall not name names or spell out actual events in recognizable detail, but I can show exactly how the process works. I have material in hand from the press which I can make use of selectively so that the version I present cannot be written off as just fiction.

Thus I cite an account of a tragic death where a bereaved wife touches the hearts of her readers by the poignancy of her story. The husband's death came suddenly and unexpectedly as a result of an accident. The bereaved wife gives such a vivid picture of her husband's last moments and his last words that one feels for her as for a friend. When her thoughts run back to the past and to how she had gotten to know the man she was to marry, the reader's heart goes out to her. The depth of her devotion to the lost husband rings touchingly through her recorded memory of their early days together. And she gives a winningly sensitive account of some of his idiosyncrasies. Memories are recalled of the little teasing touches of banter and self-mockery that made him so dear and their love so natural. Moreover, her account of the details of what followed the first moments of bereavement abounds in affection and gratitude for all who came to help and comfort her in the aftermath of the loss. This, we feel, is no self-centered person, but a woman generous in her sympathies and affections.

Yet, at the end of it all, almost in parentheses as it were, she remarks how friendly and gracious her husband's ex-wives were to her in her bereavement. Somehow this last remark makes us pause. Doubts assail us. Surely readers whose feelings are genuinely touched by a record of deep attachment, personal loss and acute suffering ought not to be asked to swallow, at the end of it all, a set of values which they cannot possibly share. Is it cruel to make this point? Should we readers be concerned when, at the end of an article overflowing with genuine love and grief, there should slide into our consciousness a few words which somehow make us emotively accessory, after the event, to a way of life which in sober moments we deplore?

It would seem unfeelingly judgmental, sanctimoniously priggish, to ask the questions which rush into the mind. How many ex-wives were there? Did the first wife really want to be divorced? Did the second wife really want to be divorced? Was this the bereaved wife's first experience of marriage? At what point in the succession of marriages did the deceased husband commence his affair with the woman now widowed? I hesitate to write the sentences I am writing. Are they not tasteless, offensive, uncharitable? Or is that hesitancy of mine a sign that I am in danger of being brainwashed by fashionable liberalism which pretends that there can be divorces without human cost, without fault on either side, without children left fatherless or motherless and without damage to them?

As readers, we don't need to know who was at fault. But neither do we want alien attitudes involving profound issues to be lightly peppered over tributes so moving as this one. Indeed, the tribute is so overpoweringly authentic that the reader is cajoled into swallowing the new ethic under the heart-rending appeal to the emotions. But when the heart is touched, the head ought not be seduced into temporarily accepting patterns of sexual relationship that are destructive of family life.

We are now up against propaganda in the media that is relentless. We can read lively pieces in the daily paper in which journalists interview media personalities, novelists and the like. We are introduced to a woman who has had perhaps a couple of children, and has then divorced their father to accommodate a lover. In consequence she is treated by the interviewer as someone worth consulting on the subject of how life should be lived. That is our real concern in this respect. Public figures, celebrated in the media and featured in large photographs in the press, establish themselves thus as role models for conduct and are presented as refreshingly up-to-date in their attitudes. Yet their views are destructive of the moral foundations of family life.

The thoughtful Christian surely cannot allow the abandonment of marriage and the family in popular thinking and popular practice to take place without resistance. Yet I find a bishop quoted as saying that moralizing is "one of the least attractive of human characteristics." I do not know how important the bishop in question considers the distinction between the moral and the immoral to be. And I do not know that our Lord sought to make himself "attractive" when he gave advice on human behavior. It is not enjoyable to moralize. We Christians know too well now that spelling out the truth in today's world is never going to win popular applause. If we measure the value of anything we say or do by its "attractiveness" we are lost souls.

The situation we face is that attitudes destructive of marriage and of family life are being pushed by the media today. And they reveal or mask determination ultimately to see the end of marriage as we have known it. We hear that the family is an institution in a state of flux. "You have to gallop to keep pace with family life, which changes so profoundly in just a few years." That is how one woman writer puts it. You have to run at top speed to be up-to-date in handling this chameleonlike institution, family life. As for marriage itself, "Nobody seems able to tell me why we're still doing it," says another.... "Surely we have the imagination to come up with something better ... than an institution that came in with the Ark." Thus for many a media person marriage and the family are already a thing of the past. "Marriage has had it," we read in a comment on its "terminal decline."

Admittedly such extreme views do not yet figure much in open public discussion. But they illustrate how the wind is blowing, as we say. And disparagement of marriage is disparagement of human fidelity. Consider how gravely marital infidelity was handled by the great Victorian novelists of the nineteenth century. Then consider how lightly many of our contemporaries treat it today. The keeping of marriage vows is now relegated to the status of a side issue in post-Christian thinking. Yet in comparable suffering may be involved. Sometimes infidelity results in stark tragedy. Within a few days I have read two tragic accounts of infidelity. One concerned an American couple. A photograph of an earnest young woman clearly experiencing emotional depths accompanied the story of how she had found in her husband's car heart-rending photographic evidence of his adultery. Under the shock of this sudden discovery, she took a gun and killed him as he lay in bed. She now faces either execution or life-imprisonment.

The other story, nearer home in England, tells how a husband became aware of his wife's infidelity with a fellow member of their sailing club. He strangled her and then cunningly suspended her body so she appeared to have hanged herself. The couple have two young children.

It seems almost improper to use instances of profound tragedy as specimens in argument, however well intentioned. But I could not escape the feeling, in reading of these murders, that the crucial acts that lay at the root of them were glossed over. Indeed, the journalist's account of this latter case speaks of the husband having strangled his wife "because he believed that she had become a social embarrassment." It sounds as though she were killed because she dropped her aitches or put potatoes into her mouth with a knife instead of a fork. Social embarrassment! The woman was secretly meeting a common friend of the couple and committing adultery in the back of his car. And, in condemning the husband, the judge declared, "You snuffed out the life of your wife entirely for your own selfish reasons without any regard for those two children." Well, yes. But ... but ... Is there no more to it than that—a selfish, callous husband ignoring the welfare of the two little children? Murder is murder, and there can be no defense, no excuse to mitigate its wickedness. That said, however, we must note that it is only in the post-Christian period that such crimes can be condemned with only the slightest peripheral attention to the initial adulteries that sparked the emotional powder keg.

Five

Marriage and Divorce

The subject of marital fidelity has been brought to my mind in a very different context. I have been very moved by Tchaikovsky's opera *Eugene Onégin*. That in itself is perhaps not surprising. It seems to have moved Tchaikovsky himself to an extraordinary degree. "Yesterday," he wrote in 1878, a year before its first performance, "I played the whole of *Eugene Onégin*.... The author was the sole listener.... The listener was moved to tears."

The opera was closely based on a narrative poem by Pushkin, a writer of the earlier years of the century, and the poem dates from 1833.

The main events in the story can be simply told. Tatyana, a romantically minded young lady living in the country, falls desperately in love when she first sees Onégin, the young heir to a neighboring estate. So desperately in love is she that she writes a letter to him, confessing all, and throws herself utterly on his mercy. When she then meets him to hear what he has to say in reply, he answers frankness with frankness, but in a cool, dispassionate way. He can feel brotherly affection for her, he says, but that is not love, and he is not the marrying type. The man's lack of sensitivity to another's plight, his unfeeling mode of rejecting her and his sheer priggishness have a devastating effect on the girl. Her mother takes her, heartbroken, to Moscow in search of change and of a husband. Eventually she is married to a friendly but dull and much older man, Count Gremin.

Six years later, after traveling abroad, Onégin meets Tatyana again at a ball in St. Petersburg. This time, he is at once overwhelmingly captivated by her beauty. Her effect on him matches in intensity his effect on her at their first encounter. He writes passionately to her as she had once written passionately to him, and in the subsequent meeting the former roles of the two as wooed and wooer are fully reversed. Onégin pleads his adoration and devotion in desperate fervor. In a deeply moving climax, Tatyana confesses that she too remains in love with Onégin, but despite all his entreaties she will remain faithful to her husband.

We need scarcely ask ourselves whether, at the close of the twentieth century, a writer could deal with marital fidelity so movingly, and know that he would carry the sympathies of the audience with him. Day after day we read in the press how this or that public figure has parted from his wife or her husband. Great sympathy is often expressed. In writing of these breakups there is in the press a new, peculiar kind of delicacy, very much a post-Christian kind of delicacy. It is a delicacy that restrains the writer from ever referring to the development except in terms of emotional strain and how it is being coped with. It is an unwritten law of journalism that in these cases no words must ever be used that might suggest there is such a virtue as fidelity and that someone must have fallen short in that respect.

Sometimes the case is such that it cries out for judgment. A man, say, for example, a writer or someone self-employed in business, may have struggled for years to make his way in life.

Through periods of struggle and stress he has been supported by the wife who was his childhood sweetheart. They may long have had to cope with financial difficulties which were the result of the husband's devotion to his work. The day arrives when the writer at last produces his best-seller or the businessman achieves his dream with a deal that gives him status and wealth. The next thing we hear is that the successful writer or business-man is parting from his wife of twenty years and living with his young secretary. "We are going to get married as soon as our divorces come through," he may say. This statement is assumed to wrap the new couple in an air of respectability.

We must not pretend that the converse development is not also far too common. A wife of many years gets restless and begins to find her husband unexciting. She works in an office or perhaps teaches in a school. Chance throws into her path a kin-dred spirit of the opposite sex, also seeking change and excite-ment. Before long she leaves her husband and shacks up with her new "partner."

When we hear or read of these cases, we learn, as a kind of afterthought, that the unfaithful husband or wife has two or three children. We are not told what the children think about it all, or what the effect has been on them. There is a conspiracy of silence surrounding such crucial matters. We hear about such matters only much later on in a very different context. A young man or a woman is before the courts for some grave offense— murder, rape or pedophilia, sometimes robbery with violence, street mugging or trading in heroin. Time after time evidence is given that the offender came from a broken home. In the back-ground there is a childhood damaged by parental divorce and a resettlement with a stepfather or a stepmother.

So far as family life and the upbringing of children is concerned we now have to face the facts. We have reached the turn of the century and the post-Christian society isn't working. It's as simple as that. But nobody is going to say so. Nobody is going to admit it. Why? Because erotic passion is assumed to be a stroke of destiny that overtakes people, overwhelms them in an irresistible tide of wholly admirable mutual devotion. That is the post-Christian estimate of erotic love. It is a god. It has its own authority. No man or woman of sincerity and generosity can resist it. There is no freedom of choice in relation to it. In comparison to its power and authority, the claims of growing children count for nothing. As for the husband or the wife from whom the new partner is being detached, they too must peaceably accept the inevitability of their loved ones' surrender to the destiny that has claimed them.

Just a few decades ago in the United Kingdom there was speculation whether a certain great actor with a worldwide reputation would be granted the knighthood that seemed to be his due. The trouble was that he had been divorced. Similarly, it has not been all that long since a query arose over whether a conservative statesman could possibly become prime minister because he had been divorced and had remarried. But a more recent case sheds light on this utterly changed attitude to divorce in its effect on public status. A senior member of the cabinet of a new government, no less than the foreign secretary Robin Cook, who, after years of marriage to a wife who has supported him through the years of rising to the top, has now, upon reaching the pinnacle of his ambitions, informed her, with considerable abruptness and discourtesy it would appear, that he is in the future to cohabit with his young secretary. The wife is a senior consultant of some standing in the medical profession, and she has not hesitated to speak with some frankness on the matter. But, as usual, the announcement that the foreign secretary is now intent on divorce from his wife and the mother of their grown children, and that he will shortly marry his new mistress,* is assumed to make the whole development publicly acceptable.

How happy is the public with this kind of thing? It is difficult to judge, but it would oversimplify the public response to say it is indifferent to the issue. Politicians and journalists repeat the mantra that a statesman's private life is a private matter, and it is by his statesmanship alone that he should be judged worthy or otherwise of his post. Of course, opposing spokespersons have suggested that a man who breaks his marriage vows so crudely is not to be trusted in public negotiation of any kind. And, indeed, we have to face the fact that the foreign minister's conduct subtly undermines the respect for authority a senior statesman ought to evoke. For while the new relationship is veiled in respectability for official occasions and in direct comment, an undercurrent of another kind emerges in gossip columns in the press. Take, for example, the headline and article that appeared in the press:

Nesting Pair

Robin Cook's search for a love nest goes on. The Foreign Secretary and Gaynor Regan, his squeeze, have been looking for the perfect *des res* in Edinburgh close to his constituency, since news of their secret liaison broke. So far the

---

*This has now happened.

lovebirds have turned their noses up at a couple of
Georgian pads in the city's New Town area....

Clearly, making heartless divorce and cohabitation superfi-
cially acceptable does not wholly silence the voice of disquiet.
Correspondingly, the dignity and authority of office are
damaged. The journalist goes out of his way to vulgarize the
relationship by his choice of words. The mistress who has sup-
planted the loyal wife becomes the foreign secretary's "squeeze."

Defenders of the new openness will rightly point out that earlier in the century the indiscretions of public figures were simply
hushed up. When Lloyd George, the prime minister who
guided the country through the First World War, treated his wife
with scant respect and took his secretary as his mistress, no journalist would have touched on the matter. Thus damage to public authority and reputation was avoided. Even a couple of
decades later, in 1936, the British press long kept a discreet
silence about the new King Edward VIII's affair with Mrs. Wallis
Simpson. When the crisis came and the story broke, the question
was raised: Could the new king get away with it? Could he marry
a twice-divorced woman and make her queen? Members of
Parliament were all but unanimous. Ramsay MacDonald, the
leader of the Labour Party, put it bluntly: "The people of this
country do not mind fornication but they loathe adultery."

One does not have to look far for attitudes toward marriage
and adultery that are very different from those of today's
Western media. I read this morning in my newspaper that a
Tehran court found a German businessman "guilty of having
sex with an unmarried 27-year-old medical student." The
Muslim woman was sentenced to ninety-nine lashes while the

German businessman is to be stoned to death. That seemingly is the appropriate punishment for adultery in Iran. I gather that about two hundred such offenders were executed in Tehran in 1997. We in the West all recoil from such savagery. But many of us recoil also from the conversely overly light treatment of adultery and family breakups that disfigure our own civilization.

If we take everything into account, is it better to be overly severe about adultery or to treat it too lightly? One hardly dares to speak logically on this issue. The post-Christian media would make a mockery of anyone who seriously tried to grapple with it. For a civlized society executing adulterers is not an option. But such laws and penalties at least attach gravity to an offense which the post-Christian mind of the West has trivialized.

There was, of course, no death penalty for adultery in the Russian society for which Pushkin wrote his poem. Nor was there a legal penalty for adultery in the Russian society for which Tchaikovsky wrote his opera. There was, however, a social penalty. Tatyana speaks of the "degradation" that was the lot of the faithless wife. Can we be sure in matters of this kind that the post-Christian mind of the late twentieth century has gotten things right? Yes, when we read of executions for adultery in the Muslim world, we can flatter ourselves that our civilized legal system has the moral edge over that which exists in Iran. But when the dramatic climax of Tchaikovsky's opera is reached and the music rises in those surging phrases that tear at the heart, what then? When we hear Tatyana nevertheless resisting the agonizingly passionate appeals of the devoted young man she has always loved, can we be sure that we know better nowadays? "Why should I lie?" Tatyana asks in response to the lover's desperate claim upon her. "Yes, I love you still." That might have marked the end of her marriage in a late twentieth-century drama. But no. She is Germin's wife. She vowed fidelity to him as his bride. She will not leave him, and she bids Onégin farewell.

Past literature abounds in stories of marital infidelity that result in tragedy. But when journalists today report contemporary cases of infidelity on the part of admired notorieties, they generally refrain from calling up memories of such historic and legendary marital breakups. We are not reminded of Helen of Troy or Anna Karenina, for such memories might predispose readers to look at things differently. That is to say, we are not seriously reminded of such cases. If they are brought to mind, it must be in fun, in mockery, in irony.

I have before me a piece about a well-known TV personality for whom a man in the media business has forsaken his wife and their three children. The journalist is a woman. She admits that in the case of the TV presenter and her stolen partner there are circumstances that intensify the injured wife's sense of wrong. Most notably, the wronged wife counted her husband's new mistress as her friend. But when the journalist begins by recalling how wronged women have reacted in the past in revenge for infidelity, the tone is clearly ironic. "Medea reacted by murdering her children, Clytemnestra butchered her husband and his mistress in the bath."* It is implied that such responses are a bit of a joke in modern eyes.

---

*Unfortunately the journalist has gotten her facts wrong. Clytemnestra, Agamemnon's wife, was the guilty party who took Aegisthus as her lover while her husband was fighting at Troy. When Agamemnon returned from the Trojan War, Clytemnestra killed him to safeguard her position. It was Orestes, her son, and his sister Electra, who killed the guilty couple, Clytemnestra and Aegisthus.

The question at issue in the piece is: How does a wronged wife get revenge while preserving her dignity? In this case the wronged wife made no dramatic protestations. But, discovering as she prepared herself for a party that her husband and his mistress were themselves to be guests, she refused to drop out and spare them possible embarrassment. Instead, she dressed and groomed herself to her best, went along to the party and danced prominently before them in seeming total self-assurance through the night. The journalist sides with the wife in not having voiced resentment through the media at the wrong done to her. But the air of semi-flippancy that over-hangs the initial comparisons with Medea and Clytemnestra sets the tone for the piece. The sensitive reader registers the great effort being made not to lapse into what would be considered old-fashioned, moralistic talk which really would call a spade a spade, adultery adultery, and treachery treachery. Yet somehow the story, as handled, calls out for it. And the reader cannot but wonder whether the three children, bereft of their father, do not deserve a mention.* The post-Christian mind allows a degree of selectivity in recording such matters. The post-Christian mind is deceptively evasive. It dare not face facts.

A new development in the attempt to endow divorce with a more dignified status has lately gained publicity. I have just read an article recommending couples to organize their divorces in such a way that they attain the kind of symbolic status a wedding has. "Parting need not be hell," we are told. "A divorce ceremony can turn it into a peaceful, even positive

---

*In actual fact, the erring husband, moved especially by love for his children, soon returned to his wife.

act." Various devices already used are described. First, we have the story of an American couple:

> For four hours they listened to each other talk about their relationship, they drank water from a glass pitcher that had been used at their wedding ceremony, they forgave each other and they buried their rings in the back garden. Finally they smashed the pitcher.

This, we are told, "enabled them to leave each other in a trusting state rather than a blaming one."

Then we hear the story of an English couple, both teachers, told in their own words.

> We took the ribbon from our wedding car, a Bentley, and tied it round ourselves in a figure of eight. Then we cut it and fell backwards away from each other. It felt like symbolically separating. It cemented a new phase of my life. It was a symbolic severing of our emotional ties that enabled us to step into a new phase and also to remain friends.

The fact that this couple has "three grown-up children" does not seem to enter into the ceremony of splitting and embarking on a new phase.

Lastly, we have the account of an English couple who "had been married for ten years and had a three-year-old son when, last year, they decided their marriage was over." Accordingly they sat together in a hot bath and this is how the wife described what happened:

Suddenly it seemed the right space. We were naked and vulnerable, so we decided to do it then and there. We sat in silence for two or three minutes just being and feeling together. It was very painful. Then we spoke about everything we'd gained from each other over the past 10 years, we apologized to each other for causing pain, and I cried buckets.

The next stage was to take off their wedding rings and to choose a plant hanging over a table that was "very precious" to them:

We placed our rings on different tendrils of the plant, which symbolized creating psychological space for each other and the giving of the greatest growth to each other.

I am not here concerned to analyze the meaningless psychobabble in all three accounts, about "just being," about trusting states and blaming states, about cementing a new phase of life and about creating psychological spaces, whatever they are. I am more concerned to make a point about the total neglect of the moral dimension and the sheer self-indulgence of the whole egocentric emphasis on transient feeling.

Moreover, there is a fact that ought to worry anyone with a sense of history and with a feeling for the human lot, not just from day to day, but from decade to decade and from century to century. It was fascinating to see how Tchaikovsky, at work in the 1870s, was able to enter into the mood of a work written by a poet fifty years earlier. Further than that, we can say that Pushkin's story would have made moral and emotional sense to the public in any civilized western European country over the previous four centuries. That public would have fully understood and empathized with the tragic sequence of events and the demand for the loyal wife, Tatyana, to make the decision she did. For over four hundred years at least, ethic would have kept its authenticity and its appeal. Those, of course, were four hundred years of Christian civilization. But in the recent accounts of attitudes to divorce we have narratives that would have seemed utterly nonsensical to our own reading public even as recently as fifty years ago. We are in a new world, a post-Christian world, a world of self-deceiving pscychobabblers from whose minds the moral laws of a whole civilization have been swept away.

Nothing, however, is more satisfying to the post-Christian mind than the ironing out of distinctions between contraries or opposites. And if divorce can be endowed with the flavor of a solemn interchange between the parties and surrounded with the trappings of symbol and ceremony, why, divorce will have become the respectable handmaid of marriage, an occasion of parallel positive significance. Aslan is Tash. Tash is Aslan.

Six

Morality Under Attack

No sooner had I finished writing the previous chapter than I read a leading article in my daily paper, *The Times*. It is headed "New Family Values." It praises the new leader of the UK Conservative Party for trying to "rid his party of one of its least attractive traits: an attachment to the priggish and sometimes prejudiced morality of the fifties and before." Now the suggestion that the moral values of all ages prior to the 1960s were "priggish" seems to me to be hair-raising. Is this one of our complaints against Shakespeare, against Dickens, against Sir Philip Sidney, against Dr. Johnson and John Wesley? Were they all brainwashed into acceptance of a priggish morality? (Notice that "prejudiced" is qualified by "sometimes," but "priggish" is not.) And what about our own personal family ancestors? Were all our grandparents prigs? From the argument pursued in the article it appears they were. For they were so misguided as to think it was wrong for women to have babies outside of marriage and by choice to bring them up on their own. They were so misguided as to judge homosexual practices immoral.

The article attacks the adherents of the old moral code "because they thought single parenthood was wrong rather than ill-advised." The writer seems to be hedging his or her bets here. If you make an "ill-advised" decision, according to my book, you make the "wrong" decision. But for this writer, between what is "wrong" and what is "ill advised" there is a great gulf fixed. It is priggish to think single parenthood wrong but proper to call it ill advised. The code so represented is a revealing one. The post-Christian mind wants to empty morality out of human relationships. There should be no mistake about that. The post-Christian cannot sin. He or she can only act ill-advisedly.

The same pussyfooting around issues of right and wrong can be detected throughout the article. Politicians, we are told, have the right to chatter away about problems of social behavior. "But they will be listened to only if they restrict themselves to talking about social damage rather than 'immorality.'" Now we are beginning to see the light. The writer wants the effects of human behavior to be measured by the standard of social damage-limitation. No hint of personal morality must enter into judgment of human behavior. And why is this view so strongly advocated? We can guess. Because traditional Christian morality is based on doctrines of free will that hold individuals to be responsible for their actions. In post-Christian thinking such responsibility is not to be assigned to single mothers,* nomadic or peripatetic fathers or cohabiting couples. The implicit downgrading of free will is significant.

We ought not to leave it at that. It is worthwhile to give careful attention to the argument that the rules of personal morality can now be appropriately superseded by the general

---

*I trust that it is not necessary here to make the point which by sheer common sense readers will already have understood. Namely that there is all the moral difference in the world between the lot of forsaken or widowed single parents and those who have opted for that role.

principle of social damage-limitation. It appears that this doctrine has become one of the cardinal precepts of post-Christian
thinking. We should note that the doctrine is one that has been
widely accepted in certain criminal circles long before it attained
the dignity of being advanced in the leading article of a supposedly serious newspaper. The principle of damage-limitation is
the principle by which thieves square their consciences when
they rob houses. "The insurance company will pay up," they
argue. "No one is harmed." That is the logic that now sustains
people in dishonest practices of a dozen different kinds. Too
many young people have been brought up to respect only the
single moral imperative that you must not harm other people,
that you must not cause pain, injury or damage to others. On a
simplistic reading of this basis you can devise methods of swin-
dling banks of millions of dollars by credit-card trickery. "It
doesn't harm anyone," the argument runs. "No individual person will really be any worse off to a noticeable degree." On the
same basis, at a more modest level of chicanery, you can hold a
paying job while drawing State benefits intended only for the
unemployed. "Who is harmed?" the culprit asks. If press reports
are to be believed, State agencies are being robbed of millions
by fraudulent claims that can be excused because they "do no
damage to anyone."

The principle has bitten so deeply into the minds of some of
our contemporaries that it has produced an astonishing recent
incident of deception which can perhaps supply us with a little
light relief. I read today of a happily married couple, both sixty-
three years old. They took such delight in their marriage service
in 1978 that, seventeen years later, in 1995, they passed themselves off as single people and had a repeat ceremony. The joy

they took in it was such that, two years later, they again posed as single people and for the third time gathered their family and friends together for the solemn ceremony at another church. Apparently their experiments turned them into addicts. And now they appear to have overreached themselves. Their fourth wedding was planned for next month, but someone blew the whistle on them. "This was going to be the last time," the good wife said apologetically. And her husband added, "It is not harming anyone." Indeed, the local registrar is so touched by the romantic aspect of the offenses that there will be no prosecution.

Let us return to the press article that urged us to use social damage-limitation as the measure of judgment on human behavior rather than ancient notions of personal morality. The writer then appeals to another code by which judgments can be made. "Cohabitation, for instance, is no longer considered by most people as living in 'sin.'" Considered by most people? In what civilizations was the basis of morality established by majority vote? It could have been truly said in Nazi Germany in the 1930s and 1940s that rounding up Jews was no longer considered by most people as improper. What does that tell us? It could be said today in certain Muslim countries that executing adulterers is not considered by most people as improper. That proves nothing at all. However, the writer of this article is so confident that the opinion of the liberal mass media in the 1990s is on target that he or she can write off countless generations of our ancestors as prejudiced prigs. It would appear that the writer has no time for the public opinion of any age except the present age. That blinded viewpoint is one that the process of education is supposed to remove at an early stage.

The whole piece reeks of evasion and the desire to reflect the views of the immoral minority who use the media for the purpose of decomposing the moral fabric of society. The writer goes so far as to grant that "it is fair for a politician to bemoan the rise in 'never-married' single mothers. Their children will lack male role models and they are likely to spend much of their life living off the State." Thus we are permitted by the post-Christians to suggest that children benefit from the role model provided by a father, but not to urge that it is improper to actively deny them that benefit. The doublespeak involved in getting away from traditional defense of the institution of marriage in order to prate about the need for role models is characteristic of the shabby decay of reason that the post-Christian mind suffers from. Politicians, and we, the general public too, it appears, are allowed to "bemoan" the consequences of human behavior but not to suggest that there was any human moral responsibility anywhere for what has happened. The implicit denial of free will is breathtaking. Citizens are to be treated as automata.

The article graciously labels the family as "one of the most successful institutions in society." This use of words once more empties evaluation of all moral content. The Mafia has been one of the "most successful" institutions in society. Stalin was one of the "most successful" statesmen of his age. So what? The writer goes on to speak of "the social and personal costs of family breakdown." Once again morality is thrown out the window. The expression "family breakdown" echoes the expression "marriage breakdown" which suggests that marriages can let couples down in the same way as their cars can. They think at first that they've got a good model but, lo and behold, it gives out on the motorway and leaves them stranded on the hard shoulder. This now popular abuse of the noun "marriage" corrupts our thinking. Instead of speaking of two free human beings who make a success of their relationship or fail, instead of speaking of two free human beings who manage to keep their solemn vows or break them, we talk about this thing "marriage" as though it were a new car or a new house. It may prove to be as good as it promised, or it may turn out to have a deficient alternator or a leaky roof. If it turns out to be OK, that's a piece of good luck. If it lets you down, that's a piece of bad luck. In either case, little or no responsibility is attached to the owner.

That is the crucial point for the post-Christian mind. Responsibility must be shifted from the shoulders of human beings. They must not be treated as creatures of free will with moral choices to make. We now have "animal rights" enthusiasts who are concerned that four-legged creatures in our midst should get a fair deal. The dignities of animal-kind, they complain, are abused in the circus and in the abattoir. No doubt they are right. But do we not need more a "human rights" movement that will protect the dignities of humankind? Let us band together to decry all post-Christian attempts to shift from human beings the God-given rights of free will. Let us have some appropriate slogans to hold before the faces of those post-Christian manipulators of word and mind who would so debase us. We demand the restoration of our freedom! We believe we are responsible for our own actions!

One of the peculiarities of post-Christian thinking is the desire to swim with the tide. It has always been thought to be an aspect of a healthy educational process to make the young suspicious of current fashions and novel developments.

Civilization cannot, of course, progress unless there is change for the better, but it will regress if the change is for the worse. The need for fresh thinking in all spheres of life and thought is accepted, but it cannot cancel out the fact that initially the young learn from the old. They inherit values and tastes just as they inherit the language they speak. In this respect it has naturally been the lot of the mature age groups to rein in the experimentation of the young when it seems to threaten moral and cultural stabilities that have stood the test of time. What is peculiar about the current post-Christian climate of thinking is that the mature age groups seem frightened of handing on to the young the values that they themselves inherited—and benefitted from.

Thus the notion that those in authority should be especially wary of setting an example that might damage the young has been jettisoned. In the United Kingdom this year we have seen a cabinet minister abruptly leave his wife and begin to cohabit with his young secretary. In the same period we have seen the leader of the Opposition party attending the party's annual conference and openly cohabiting with his fiancée in the conference hotel. Now, not surprisingly perhaps, we have the chairman of the Society of Headmasters and Headmistresses of Independent Schools tackling this issue at the society's annual conference. He has openly criticized the cabinet minister and the leader of the opposition for their flouting of moral standards. "Who is taking the moral lead?" he asked. "With the erosion of the nuclear family it all too often seems to come down to schools and their teachers in isolation." It is a very fair comment. Trying to bring up the young with moral standards that include respect for marriage and family life is obviously far harder when all can see the spectacle of people at the top setting so bad an example. We might add, too, it is made worse when all can read newspaper leading articles such as the one that sparked off this exploration of current attitudes.

The leading article under consideration can throw further light on the workings of the post-Christian mind. We should note that the article is headed "New Family Values," when in fact the gist of much of the reasoning is to recommend acceptance of practices of cohabitation and homosexuality which are destructive to the family. Clearly "New Anti-Family Practices" would have been a more appropriate heading. But we have seen that it is not the habit of most post-Christian propagandists to make frank statements such as "The family has had its day." Instead practices inimical to the preservation of the family are recommended under the specious label "New Family Values." The advantage of this technique is that the healthy emotional associations held by the word "family" can be surreptitiously transferred to practices that destroy the family.

I was once familiarly acquainted with a rural area of England through which a very minor railway ran from village to village. It was said, jokingly, that cows were not allowed to die natural deaths on the farms adjacent to the railway line. For if an aged or ailing cow could be induced to stray through a broken hedge onto the railway track and be killed by a passing train, then compensation for its death could be claimed from the railway's insurance company. This story provided amusing party chatter. Perhaps there were actual events to corroborate it. I do not know. I only know that no one wrote an article defending the dishonest practice under the heading "New Honesty Values." There may have been wicked relish of wickedness, but no one tried to claim that this was what the insurance industry was now all about. No one said, "This practice does no social damage to society."

More profound than the issue raised by this manipulation of language is the issue raised by the article's implicit philosophy that political leaders must carefully register what the popular trend is, and then follow it (or rather, pretend to lead it). Now we must accept that politicians in a democratic society are supposed to operate in accordance with the will of the voters. More must be said about that theory elsewhere. Here we must only note that testing public opinion can never be a basis for moral judgment. We have cited already the masscorruption of public opinion in Nazi Germany. Yet at several points in the article that we are studying the appeal to public opinion is basic. "The majority of people born after the war ... share a certain set of attitudes." "Liberally-inclined voters will become an ever-increasing element of the electorate. Any party that tried to shut its eyes to this demographic trend would be condemning itself to electoral oblivion."

It may be just and proper for a political party to adjust its economic or welfare policy to the demands of the electorate. But to try to adjust moral principles to the prevailing wind in public-opinion surveys is not only to abdicate from leadership but also to abandon all integrity. And yet, is not this development the natural consequence of the loss of faith? The post-Christian mind has lost those transcendent foundations for the regulation of conduct which only a religious affiliation can supply. This tragic deprivation in post-Christian statesmen may be concealed as they talk of public policy in a thousand different contexts. But once they enter the field of moral behavior, then the threadbare character of their moral thinking will be revealed. No one can turn moral issues into matters that public-opinion polls can determine.

There are two basic directions in which human judgment operates. Let us try to differentiate them at their simplest and crudest. You may say, "This garden covers two acres" or "This garden is beautiful." The one statement is a quantitative judgment. The other statement is a qualitative judgment. We judge in terms of quantity, citing measurements and dimensions. We also judge in terms of quality, citing aspects that deserve approval or disapproval. No values are involved in making quantitative judgments. To say "The house is small" is not necessarily to depreciate the house any more than to say "The garden is large" is necessarily to praise the garden. A purchaser may be seeking a large house with a small garden or vice versa. According to the purchaser's particular needs the quantitative judgment may assume a qualitative aspect, but this is not inherent in the bare statement.

The post-Christian mind tends to escape from argument in terms of quality to argument in terms of quantity. That is exactly what the writer of the article we are studying does. Deprived of the capacity to reason in terms of what is good or bad, the writer falls back on claiming numerical preponderance for the views he or she is propagating. "The majority of people" and "most people" have this or that attitude. Both expressions ought to serve as a warning signal to the reader that argument in terms of good or evil, right or wrong, is to be abandoned in favor of appeals to supposed numerical preponderance.

Thus it is not surprising that the writer is scathing of Christian views that seem "to emanate from moral absolutism."

Here the writer seems to give the word "absolutism" the pejorative connotation which it has acquired from use in the political field as descriptive of tyrannous oppression. There is, of course, no escape from the clarity of moral definition which the writer seemingly rejects except to moral relativism. Either good is good and evil is evil, or our human system of reasoning can have no reliable basis. In fact, what the post-Christian mind hates most in Christians is that morally they know where they stand and that the positions they cling to are corroborated by centuries of experience.

Quantitative reasoning is the basis of market research. In such areas it is no doubt useful to ask the question, "How many people tend to purchase this or that commodity?" Quantitative reasoning is also the basis of the insurance industry: "What is the statistical likelihood that this man or this woman will survive to be seventy or eighty?" "What is the statistical likelihood that this insured's car will be wrecked in a crash?" "What is the statistical likelihood that this house will be destroyed by fire?" While we are involved in the material business of life, as shoppers or retailers, as consumers or producers, we are continually making quantitative judgments. While we are busy with practical matters of spending and saving, looking after our homes and our families, the need is there for calculation of loss and gain, of what this or that requirement will cost and what can be afforded. Our thinking is daily threaded with reference to the tables of mental arithmetic or to the pocket calculator.

In the sphere of the quantitatively calculable "the most" and "the least" stand at opposite ends of the scale of judgment. In the sphere of the qualitatively calculable "the best" and "the worst" stand at opposite ends of the scale of judgment. In the post-Christian environment of today more and more matters of living experience which demand qualitative judgment are being subsumed within the dominion of the quantitatively measurable. Thus our writer was prepared to argue a case on the basis of what "most people" believe and what "the majority of people" do. Instead of asking what is the ideal for human behavior, the post-Christian wants to know what is the prevailing average of human behavior. The tyranny of the average holds the post-Christian mind in its grip.

Seven

Values

We have been dealing with views publicly expressed under the heading "New Family Values." The views, when examined, turned out to be hostile to the family as we understand it. The word "values" was introduced, as it often is nowadays, merely to present views destructive of Christian principles under a veil of respectability. I have just heard someone speaking on the radio about the "changing values" of modern life. The speaker was referring to the fact that some conduct that was considered improper in our grandparents' days is now treated as respectable. One has to choose words carefully here. Conduct once considered improper but now "treated" as respectable is not necessarily universally considered as really worthy. An obvious instance is the way in which a man and a woman may today set up an establishment together and have children without marrying, indeed, seemingly without contemplating the possibility of marriage. We have to accept that many of those who publicly "treat" such couples as respectable may have private reservations about their conduct. The post-Christian mind, however, appears to accept that the ready availability of contraceptives, more or less reliable, has enabled men and women to change their notions of what is good and what is bad in human behavior. The speaker regarded this development as evidence of "changing values."

But do "values" change in respect to human conduct? Certainly values seem to change in respect to material objects. An Impressionist painting that was once regarded as of little worth may change hands in the art market today for millions of dollars. But would the artist who painted the picture accept that the "value" of his painting had escalated over the years? Would he not distinguish what he might call the "true value" of the work from the current market value at any given time? After all, there is a market value for goods which is determined by their relative scarcity or abundance. When we turn from considering such things as paintings and houses, antiques and bottles of old wine, and begin to consider aspects of human behavior, then clearly the connotation of the word "value" changes too. Most of us would accept that honesty is a moral value to be encouraged and admired in human conduct. But that value cannot be expressed on a sliding scale according to the relative prevalence of honest people in your neighborhood. An honest man is an honest man, and, although his honesty might shine out vividly if he lived among a pack of thieves and therefore had a rarity rating in his environment, he could not claim to be "more honest" than the honest man who lived among honest men.

Is it not wholly illogical to bring to bear upon our consideration of human behavior a sliding scale of valuation? We turn to the financial pages of our daily newspaper to discover whether electricity shares are worth more or less than they were worth yesterday. The Financial Times Index and the Dow Jones Index register overall improvement or deterioration in stock market valuations from day to day. When I hear people talking about the "changing values" in human relationships and human conduct I am tempted, as a Christian, to picture a similar record being kept. It would go like this: "The Moral Market Today. Chastity is down three points and Honesty is up two points. The chartists foresee a further surge in Honesty as the moral climate becomes increasingly indulgent toward admissions of conduct that would once have been regarded as disgraceful or shameful. By the same token shares in Chastity, which today reached a new low, are expected to fall much further yet. All the experts agree that the bottom has fallen out of the Chastity market. Investors will be wise to rid their portfolios of this now discredited commodity before it is too late."

The serious point here is that, in the moral sphere, values do not change. What changes is the ability of men and women to live up to those values. It will be argued in reply that in twentieth-century Western countries people seem to be more compassionate to the poor and afflicted in their midst than their ancestors were in the sixteenth century. And it will be urged that in the Middle Ages cruelties were widespread— sometimes even committed in the name of Christianity—which would not be tolerated today. But we judge such variations only on the basis of unchanging standards. Compassion is compassion in every age whether a given age is deficient in it or not. Charity is charity in every age, whether people practice it or turn their backs on it. It is only by virtue of a commonly accepted standard of charity or compassion that we can pass judgment on acts of cruelty that betray that standard.

The words "commonly accepted standard" introduce us to another aspect of bad thinking in current usage which nourishes the post-Christian mind. I read in a newspaper that "the

Christian has no right to impose his private values on others."
Can there possibly be such a thing as a "private value"? Strictly
speaking, no. The expression is a contradiction in terms. The
value of anything unless it is in the public purview is not something that lends itself to logical discussion. A widow may justly
say of a photograph of her dead husband, "Its value is priceless
to me." But, for purposes of rational argument, is that not the
same thing as saying, "I set such importance on this photograph that I exempt it from all generally applicable systems of
valuation"? Insofar as the photograph has a special value for the
widow, it is a value that defies all scales of valuation. In other
words, here, where there might appear to be something that
amounts to a "private value," it turns out to be significant primarily as a refutation of all public valuations. You would not
find the post-Christian journalist protesting in the press that
the widow is trying to impose her "private values" on others
when she insists on the uniquely precious character of the
photograph. The truth is that the real value at issue in the
widow's declaration is the value of fidelity to her dead husband
and love of her dead husband. Neither fidelity nor love could
be called a "private" value, however personal and particular an
individual's practice of these virtues may be.

A value has the normative status of a standard of measurement by reference to which judgments can be made. Such standards can function only insofar as they are publicly recognized.
A man might invent a private system of linear measurement to
replace yards and feet, meters and centimeters. But he would
be able to explain it to others only by reference to a prevailing
system of measurement publicly accepted. If I invent a new
scale of my own, it will be incomprehensible to anyone else

unless I refer it back to the publicly accepted norms. "My new unit is the 'derm,' which is divided into ten 'deciderms.' The derm is one foot three inches long and therefore the deciderm is exactly an inch and a half." The private scale is intelligible only when it is converted into a public scale.

We have heard too much lately about Christians trying to impose their "private" values on a secular society. And from time to time in this book we turn up evidence of concepts produced by psychobabblers that the post-Christian mind is happy to pass off as "values." Here and now, however, we must insist that "private" morality, unless it means an individual's personal and particular application of universal morality, is a contradiction in terms. All morality is public. A person's moral system could be limited to being "private" only insofar as it was distinguishable from other people's, but a code of conduct strictly inapplicable to anyone else would not be a code at all but a collection of whims. If a given attitude is distinguishable from any attitudes adopted by others, it cannot be described as moral. There is, of course, a moral code that is recognizably "Christian," but in no sense is it private. On the contrary, it has universal application to the whole of humanity. As for imposing that moral code on the public in general, Western civilization has, by and large, established its judicial system and its code of law on the basis of Judeo-Christian formulations.

Christians today need to be perpetually vigilant against the central assault of post-Christian secularism. The assault takes the form of an attempt to relativize whatever is fixed, whatever is firm, whatever represents the absolute and the transcendent in the presuppositions on which Christian civilization has been built. It is necessary to remind ourselves continually that the post-Christian agenda is for the destruction of morality by process of decomposition. That is to say, recognized stabilities— whether spiritual, intellectual or moral—must be undermined. Whatever the Christian accepts as universally true, valid, binding and decisive must be rendered in appearance a matter of conjecture or opinion, of choice or whim, of variable relevance or application, of ultimately subjective significance only.

A curious by-product of the relativization of morality is worth mentioning here. It is a peculiar development notable in well-to-do, middle-class circles. There are people who adopt a pose of flippancy in relation to grave moral injunctions. Thus the prohibitions listed in the Ten Commandments can readily be handled with a frivolous air of knowing superiority. The attitude is that such prohibitions oversimplify the subtleties of personal behavior now more fully understood in the age of psychiatry. Up to a point this attitude may do little harm. Mockery of moral principles lightly expressed with a sherry glass in hand at a party, or decorated with humor in the journalist's gossip column, may indeed not count for much. Moralists can afford to shrug off the clever-clever gibes of the sophisticated ironists.

But what if word turns into deed? What if the clever-clever scorn of sober moral precept becomes active? I have just read a press piece examining the behavior of a new kind of thief. There are well-to-do shoplifters who help themselves to goods in stores just for the fun of it. Two cases are cited. The one is a university graduate with a well-paid job in marketing. She is thirty-five, lives prosperously and is engaged to be married. She confesses that she goes to the local store on a Saturday morning on a shoplifting expedition. "It makes me laugh so much," she says. "I'm like a gleeful child." Another woman, a literary agent in the same social class, enjoys the same kind of fun. Neither steals items they could not afford to pay for.

It is clearly not difficult to pick up things, pop them in a bag and leave the store paying only for chosen items. If you are discovered and you are the kind of person who can well afford to pay for the goods, your explanation that it was all a mistake will apparently see you through with only a mild warning to be more careful in the future. It is not well-dressed, well-spoken, clearly affluent middle-class ladies who are likely to be pounced on by store detectives. It is individuals seemingly more open to temptation. What is interesting in the psychology of these people is that they mentally inhabit a post-Christian world in which theft can be laughed off.

One of secularism's most useful devices for weakening the Christian Church has been the policy of relativizing and individualizing values and beliefs. I think an important Christian defense against this policy is for us to be on our guard against allowing people to mentally write off our Christian convictions as purely individual hunches. Our belief in the resurrection of Christ is not an interesting personal preference on a par with our fondness for colorful ties or detective novels. Such articles of belief are the universal endowment of a massive body of humanity stretching back through the centuries and reaching forward into eternity. When I was active in the academic world, I was sometimes asked questions such as, "What is your opinion?" or "What do you think?" in relation to queries about fundamental religious or moral issues. And I sometimes chose to begin my reply by saying, "Look, it doesn't matter much what my opinion is or what I think." Then I could continue, "The Christian faith is that..." or "The Church teaches that..." or

"The Bible tells us that..." We have to combat the idea that great doctrines of the faith are private possessions that we acquire individually. In the same way we have to combat the idea that moral standards fundamental to good living are privately selected and amassed. People speak nowadays as though individuals have to collect a personal portfolio of morals and values to serve them through life. It is as though we have to choose and arrange together a variety of ingredients from the moral values stall and devise our own personal menu.

I heard an exchange on the radio a few days ago. It was being argued that thirteen-year-old girls ought to be given contraceptives to combat the rise in teenage pregnancies. (The old-fashioned moralist cannot but observe that every relaxation of old moral rigidities in this direction has in fact had completely the opposite effect.) The expert pressing this case was questioned about the morality of this move. The question was treated like a relic of long-discredited superstition. "Morals have moved on," she replied, as though a moral code was a kind of traveling circus, here today and gone tomorrow. This concept is really quite absurd. But the post-Christian mind is only too happy to visualize morality so. What is absolute and fixed must be rendered relative, changing and mobile. What is universal and objective must be rendered individual and subjective.

From a recent issue of *Christianity Today* we learn that the Massachusetts Supreme Judicial Court has ruled that a divorced father must stop imposing his religious beliefs on his three children. The children now live with his divorced wife, who is Jewish, and, indeed, the divorce is partly attributed to the former husband's conversion to Christianity. The Court ruled that the father "had 'substantially harmed' the children by putting his religious beliefs above their well-being." Now we must accept that this is not a straightforward case because two religious faiths are involved. Nevertheless, the official vocabulary here is characteristic of the attitudes we are up against. It is "his" religious beliefs against "their" well-being. Our Lord called Matthew from his work as a tax-gatherer, but we would not say that Christ put his personal religious beliefs before Matthew's career, still less before Matthew's "well-being." What was at issue was not our Lord's religious beliefs but Matthew's religious beliefs and, of course, closely wrapped up in that, Matthew's true "well-being."

In our Lord's mind it was necessary to Matthew's well-being that he should become his disciple. In the mind of the divorced father it was necessary to the well-being of the children that they should become Christ's followers. The notion of a conflict between one man's religious beliefs and the "well-being" of those he is anxious to convert virtually reduces the status of religious belief to the level of a kind of medicinal treatment which, if applied where it is inappropriate, will "harm" rather than cure. We are back to the concept of a person's beliefs as a mixture concocted to meet an individual's peculiar condition. If the right mixture is prescribed then the patient may do well. If the wrong mixture is prescribed then the patient's condition will deteriorate. The Christian concept of a universal, all-saving creed divinely established to meet the crying needs of the human condition is a hypothesis unacceptable to the post-Christian mind. It is something by which the young could be "substantially harmed."

Eight

The Old and the New

There is a third train of thought in the leading article I have quoted which usefully illustrates an aspect of post-Christian thinking. The writer urges people to forget the past. That section of the population, we are told, that holds to the traditional attitudes toward marriage and the family is aging and belongs to history. They cling to "Victorian values" that the younger generation has rejected. This is the general drift of the argument. So far as social mores are concerned, the young are right and the old are wrong. The argument is in keeping with the assumption that new trends must be acknowledged and encouraged. It is an aspect of the fatal belief in inevitable progress which has so disfigured popular twentieth-century thinking.

I recall a conversation I once heard among a group of young students. One of them was an African and the rest were British. The British students were probing the African about church worship in his home country. Was it true, they asked him, that churches were packed in his native land? Yes, it was. And were not the worshipers youthful on the whole? Yes, they were indeed. Then was it not depressing to go to church in England and find the churches occupied by the aged and the middle-aged while younger people were scarce? The African student shook his head and smiled. "On the contrary. I find this most encouraging. It is true that our churches at home are often full of lively young people. But when I come here, I see the evidence that Christian belief survives the years of youthful exuberance and supports people to the end of their lives."

This recollection comes back to me when I read or hear talk of how important it is to attract the young to Christian worship and how this can only be done by substituting pop music and guitars for traditional hymns and organs. The motive is seemingly a worthy one. "Let us make our worship 'relevant' (blessed word) to modern youth." And, indeed, modern youth get wildly excited in the world of discos and rock groups. Study photographs in the press of rows and rows of young people rapturously acclaiming the latest idol of the pop world. In that environment exultant youth abounds. But what about their elders? Where are they? The audience is all but devoid of them. Do we want to see this repeated in our churches? Do we want a brand of Christian worship from which mature men and women drop off by the thousands as they grow into sober adulthood? It would seem that some of our clergy do. They appear not to have experienced what so many families know all about—the way the adolescent who keeps a feverish eye on the pop charts and chases after the latest appropriate CDs and cassettes can develop into the classical music enthusiast when taste matures and childish things are put away.

The collision between the supporters of what is established and the supporters of what is novel bedevils many areas of life. Some industries depend for their survival on regular propagation of what is novel—the fashion industry, for instance. Each season there must be clothing for young ladies that catches the eye by its sheer unexpectedness, its immediately evident differentness from the vogue of yesterday. Now it is true that very often the inspiration for a given change in fashion derives from studying the modes of the past—the 1920s, the 1930s, the 1940s and so on. And indeed fashion designers will achieve novelty by imitating designs familiar in Turkey or Polynesia, ancient Egypt or Babylon. But the key to success appears to be the production of totally unpredictable novelties. The adjective "original" is thrown about as a term of maximum approval for the latest concepts of the designers.

Yet there are areas of life today in which novelty is seemingly frowned upon by commerce. I have been looking at a brochure from a travel firm advertising packaged holidays. Recommendations for hotels push claims for what is long-standing. One tempts the reader because it offers the "traditions of another age" and another, dating from the Georgian age, claims credit for "retaining its original charm." Not its original plumbing, of course, but its original charm. Then again another hotel claims to be "rich in history and tradition" and "dates back to coaching days." Even so, hotels boast of retaining a traditional atmosphere, of offering traditional hospitality, and even more forcefully of providing traditional cooking. Novelty seems to be at a discount here. "Traditional" is apparently a word rich in attractive associations when it is applied to hospitality food or even holiday atmosphere. If you examine the packets and bottles of food and drink in your pantry, you will find an extraordinary number of the products claiming to be "traditional," sometimes even sporting a seventeenth- or eighteenth-century date in large letters to draw especial attention to the long lineage.

In a certain town in the United States, I noted, within a few minutes one day, advertisements for "old-fashioned country-style bacon," for "old-style beer" and, believe it or not, for "old-time auto service."

The last instance is surely very intriguing. The adjective "traditional" or the adjective "old" may reek with warm associations in some contexts. In the first scene of Goldsmith's comedy *She Stoops to Conquer,* Mr. Hardcastle tells his wife, "I love everything old—old friends, old times, old manners, old books, old wine." We can sympathize with the sentiments. Expressions such as "old friends" and "old times" carry rich overtones. But "old-time auto service"? The mind boggles. Will the mechanics look in the trunk for the starting handle? I'm not sure that we really want "old-time" car servicing.

There is a serious point here. Businessmen who run hotels and grocery stores, restaurants and even garages are apparently convinced that descriptions such as "old-fashioned," "old-style," "old-time" and "traditional" are surefire terms of attraction, appealing to something deep in the heart's sensitivities. Yet there is now a tendency in the Christian churches, even those steeped in history and rich in the culture of the past, to ape the crude idolatry of novelty that marks the fashion industry and the world of pop music. Are some of our clergy making a terrible mistake? Is the rush to embrace current trends a strategic blunder? If they had appealed to the experts, would the church authorities have been told by the market consultants that the psychological thrust of any publicity ought to be the very opposite of what many of them have been inclined to adopt? "Visit your local church whose rites and atmosphere are rich in history and tradition. Join in prayers and worship which date back to coaching days and earlier. Savor the old liturgy. Sing the old-time hymns."

There is, of course, a much more serious matter at issue here than the question of what will attract worshipers. The idolatry of changing fashion is an aspect of post-Christian thinking that ought not to be allowed to infiltrate Christian communities and infect the Christian Church. The Church is the guardian of a stable faith resistant to fleeting fashions, intellectual and social.

> Change and decay in all around I see,
> O Thou who changest not, abide with me.

In England this is what the newly bereaved still clamor to sing at funerals of their nearest and dearest. At such points of crisis they cling to what is stable and changeless. Maybe there have been periods of history when long lifetimes could be lived in stable environments. We have our village centers that have remained to a quick glance largely untouched over the centuries. But how many of the older generation these days can go back to where they were born and brought up without encountering a totally transformed environment? The strength of the Christian Church lies in the essential changelessness of what it stands for. This stability, which transcends the changing fashions of the passing centuries, and even more the changing fashions of the passing decades, ought to be one of the dominant features that the worshiper encounters within the walls of a church. It is the world at its worldliest that makes fashion a god and forever seeks after novelty.

It is ironic that while the Church tends to de-traditionalize its message and its methods, the world of industry seems anxious to pick up the neglected vocabulary of true religion and use it to enhance the appeal of its products. In a piece in *Christianity Today,* Charles Colson drew attention to some specimens such as the advertisement for the Volvo as "A car that can help save your soul" and an IBM TV advertisement that showed nuns walking to vespers and talking about surfing the net. It has been suggested that "spirituality is in" in the advertising world, and not only in the United States. I have just seen a glossy-colored advertisement for paper, headed "It's a Sign" in gothic script, and proclaiming the message "Behold! The King of Paper is born" and "Every kind of paper to make all your communications divine." Indeed, the product is presented as "Born-Again Paper."

The question we are grappling with here is the age-old question of the proper relationship between the Church and the world. Does the Church exist to convert and refine the world? Or does it exist to water down its faith and practice until the post-Christian world can embrace it as its own? I have been to Anglican services at which I repeatedly had to ask myself the question, "Is this really Christian worship, or have I strayed into a disco?" There are times when the secularization of so-called worship by the idioms of the entertainment world verges on the blasphemous. There are mercifully also moments when one can feel that resistance to total secularization of Christian faith and practice is still alive.

It is Sunday morning and I have just listened to a service on the radio. The radio service was broadcast from Wales. The idiom was traditionally Anglican. The hymns were from the best of eighteenth- and nineteenth-century hymnology. Psalm number one was chanted in the prayer book version. The choir sang an anthem by Ernest Bullock, a worthy composer of our own century. A Welsh piece was rendered by three female voices accompanied by a harp. The sermon was meaty, coherently put together and beautifully delivered. It happened to be on the very topic I am writing about—the theme of change and changelessness. The proper claims of change were presented in terms of the Christian call to penitence and renewal. The proper status of changelessness was presented as the character of the God we worship. Everything about the whole sequence had the dignity, the simplicity, the solemnity and the phases of exuberance that are proper to worship. At no point did one have to ask oneself, "Is this a church service or a bar-room entertainment?"

Of course, this was Wales. And it has for long been my view that the Celtic nations—the Welsh, the Scots and the Irish—have a feeling for Christian faith and practice which the English lack. It seems to me there is an Anglo-Saxon allergy to religious belief which the Celts do not share. The cynic might say, "So much the better." For the cynic might argue that religious apathy saves the English from the kind of controversy that has bedeviled life in Ireland.

This issue is raised here because worship has become one of those areas where the proper distinction between the ethos of the Church and the pull of the contemporary world has been increasingly ignored. The post-Christian mind, as I keep saying, does not want differences, distinctions, categories, frameworks. It wants to submerge everything in the general flux that marks the Age of Aquarius. Just as it wants to equate the one-parent family and the two-parent family, just as it wants to equate "stable relationships" with married partnerships, just as it wants to equate homosexual practices with healthy married life, so it also wants to equate the worship of the Church with any old coming-together for entertainment and celebration. Chop away everything that makes it different and the thing can be gradually destroyed. That is true whether you are talking about marriage, the family, the moral law, Christian doctrine or the worship of the Church. Scatter the frameworks of definition. Merge the idiom of liturgy into the idiom of journalism. Merge meaty hymnology into the vapid drivel of the rock lyricists. Merge Bach and Handel into the raucously repetitive bump and wail of the pop scene.

This is the way of abdication from Christian responsibility. Not all branches of the Christian Church inherit a literary and musical tradition as rich as the Church of England's. It should be cherished. Nothing has been more horrifying for churchmen in the last few decades than the sheer arrogance with which unthinking clergy have thrown overboard the works of forerunners, literary and musical, who have enriched the life of the nation.

The worship of novelty that has so possessed the clergy of our day is not itself new. Shakespeare observed this human weakness long ago in *Troilus and Cressida*.

> One touch of nature makes the whole world kin,
> That all with one consent praise new-born gawds,
> Though they are made and moulded of things past,
> And give to dust, that is a little gilt,
> More laud than gilt o'er-dusted.

That sums up this particular human weakness. It is a weakness common to our whole race, Shakespeare tells us, that we all praise the latest thing however worthless. This in spite of the fact that the latest thing is the product of what went before it. We value the new but worthless item, with its veneer of gilt, more than we value the real gold item that has acquired through age a coating of dust. As he so often does, Shakespeare sums up an aspect of human nature unforgettably.

The worship of novelty is closely related to belief in inevitable progress. The assumption that the new will be better than the old follows naturally from that presupposition. The extraordinary thing is that it survives in the face of irresistible evidence from every auction room that in a dozen departments of life the new just cannot match the old. Where is the instrument maker who can produce a violin to match those made by Antonio Stradivari three hundred and fifty years ago? Where is the writer of today who can be classed with Shakespeare, Dante or Homer? No body of people ought to be more sensitive to the value of the old than the Christians of today—we who, in the Church of England for instance, have seen the greatest works of literature cast in the dustbin in favor of the products of literary barbarism? That is not too strong a term to use of the *New English Bible* and the *Alternative Service Book*. The good God gave the English nation three golden masterpieces of literature: the *King James Bible*, Cranmer's *Book of Common Prayer* and the plays of Shakespeare. It was indeed prudent of the Almighty, having entrusted two of them to the English clergy, to put the other in the hands of the English theater.

The worship of novelty is perhaps the most worldly of all worldly weaknesses. It has brought sadness to countless thousands of faithful Christians to see how the clergy of the Anglican Church have sought to be more worldly than the world in the mangling of long-prized modes of worship. The post-Christian mind is very much alive in the Synod, in the bishops' palaces and in the vicarages of our land.

Nine

Discrimination

"Discrimination" is today a much used word. In the past to exercise "discrimination" has properly meant to distinguish clearly and appropriately between differing objects or people. It has always been high praise to declare someone to be a person of "great discrimination." It might be that the person in question was interested in literature or some branch of art. Whatever the subject, bringing "discrimination" to bear upon it would be to bring good taste and reliable judgment to bear. To fail to distinguish between the qualities of a valuable painting by an Old Master and a bogus imitation would be a failure in artistic discrimination. To be unable to distinguish between a Chippendale chair and a modern reproduction would also be a failure of discrimination in a specialist field. To fail to recognize that a violin was not a genuine Stradivarius but a fake would be a failure of discrimination in another specialist field. At a less specialized level, where rare expertise is not required, the exercise of proper discrimination is a matter of sheer common sense.

To fail to distinguish appropriately between, say, a man and a woman, and thereby to treat them as though they were exactly and in all respects identical beings, would be a failure of proper discrimination. To fail to distinguish clearly between the

93

needs of a disabled man who had lost his legs and those of a fully healthy one would similarly be a failure to discriminate appropriately. It is necessary to say this because in recent years the words "discriminate" and "discrimination" have been used almost exclusively in a pejorative sense. In spite of that my latest dictionary defines "discriminate" thus: to single out a particular person, group, etc., for special favor or special disfavor. The dictionary notes that the word "discriminate" is usually followed by either "in favor of" or "against." It is a pity that the word has lost all neutrality and must thus involve taking sides.

True discrimination is not about abolishing distinctions, it is about establishing them. If you ensure that there is a sloping ramp as well as a flight of steps at the entry to a building so that disabled people in wheelchairs can move in and out just as unafflicted people do, that is an act of true discrimination. It recognizes the difference between people who can walk and people who cannot, and it makes appropriate and different provisions for them. This produces something like a semblance of equality between the disabled and the unafflicted. Only by the exercise of true discrimination can you put the two groups on a level footing in this respect.

Why all this talk about the meaning of the word "discrimination"? Because the post-Christian mind's current obsession with ironing out proper distinctions has become a cloak for grave attacks on morality. The principle is established that there must be no "discrimination" between persons on the grounds of race, gender or even what is misleadingly called "sexual orientation" when people are applying for jobs. The notion is encouraged that the principle of freedom requires tolerance of sexual deviance in situations where it can be dangerous.

I read in my newspaper today that an American appeals court has declared the Boy Scout movement's ban on homosexuals to be illegal. A scoutmaster in New Jersey was dismissed from his position when he admitted he was homosexual. The grounds were that the young man had violated the scout oath to remain "morally straight." It appears that other cases challenging the Scout movement's ban are pending. The appeals court took it upon itself to rebuke a judge in an earlier trial for calling the scoutmaster an "active sodomist." But surely if he was, he was. By definition, that is what many a protesting homosexual claims to be. However, the appeals court ruled that the ban on homosexuals in the Scout movement violated the state's nondiscrimination laws.

This judgment, of course, is the reasoning of topsy-turvydom. It is a gross interference with individual liberty to forbid a group of like-minded people to form an association dedicated to upholding such principles as those which are at stake here. No one is compelled to join the Boy Scouts. Application to join any such association presupposes that the applicant is in sympathy with its aims and principles. The ethic of the Boy Scout movement demands that the boys joining it should be brought up in a morally healthy environment. In the ages when common sense was brought to bear upon such matters, the issue could never have been raised.

I do not want to be alarmist, but the threat to freedom here is truly diabolical. Developments of this kind threaten to bring in an age of lunacy. Moreover, it will be an age of appalling totalitarianism. For I foresee that in another decade or so, it may well be that I should be prosecuted for making the statements I have made in this book. To deny that the homosexual environment is a "morally healthy" one will be to invite charges under legal prohibitions of discrimination. The homosexual lobby is an increasingly powerful one. Homosexual influence in the media is brainwashing the public to accept an equivalence between the homosexual and the heterosexual in all respects. The time may well come when the sections in the Epistles of Paul, not to mention certain sentences in the Old Testament, will be legally censored as unfit for publication.

Incidentally, here is another area where changes in verbal habits register propaganda victories for the post-Christian mind. Let us consider the use of the word "heterosexual." It is not in my *Oxford Dictionary*. At the front of the dictionary I read: "Third edition 1944; Reprinted with corrections 1947." There are over seventy words beginning with the prefix "hetero," and "heterosexual" is not among them. Why? Because the dictionary clearly represents the thinking of a period in which the compound would have seemed absurd. For the word "sex" and the word "sexual" are defined in terms of male and female: "...the distinction between male and female" and "...relative to the physical intercourse between the sexes." What else, on this basis, can "sexual" relationships be but relationships between the sexes? Thus, although the dictionary certainly defines "homosexual" as "having a sexual propensity for persons of one's own sex," it sees no cause to qualify the word "sexual" for general purposes. Once you make a practice of qualifying the adjective "sexual" by turning it into "heterosexual," you imply that heterosexuality is but one variant of sexuality, of which homosexuality is another variant. The standard has gone. The norm has disappeared. What was once a deviation from healthy sexuality has become a variant as acceptable as the former norm.

Hence we arrive at the absurd expression "sexual orientation," a concept which suggests that individuals have a range of possibilities before them as they consider what is to be the object for satisfaction of their sexual drives. Shall it be a person of the opposite sex or of his or her own sex? Shall it be a little boy or a little girl? Shall it be a four-legged animal or a corpse? All these have been known to give sexual satisfaction to individuals in the past. Once the individual impulse toward sexual satisfaction by means of this or that object is labeled a "sexual orientation," it is thereby put in the same category as the normal sexual desires of men and women.

There is, indeed, a "sexual orientation" that drives men to smother women in the act of raping them. Yet nowadays, we are told, no applicant for a given job must have his or her "sexual orientation" taken into account when his or her fitness for a job is weighed. Not if he is a pederast and seeks a job in a children's home? Not if he finds sexual satisfaction in corpses and is seeking a job in a cemetery or a home for geriatric residents?

The battle for morality and reason is often lost or won when a new verbal usage is accepted or rejected. We hear talk of "one-parent families" or "single-parent families" and we fail to register openly the query that lurks at the back of our minds. We join in conversation where the words "heterosexual" and "homosexual" are bandied about, and we fail to recognize that we have yielded ground in giving the two concepts a comparable status.

Moral theologians quite properly insist that the sins of the flesh are not the most dangerous of sins for the human soul.

Because that is so we hesitate to pass judgment where our Victorian ancestors would have been bluntly hostile to departures from conventional monogamous practices. We recall how secretly Dickens had to conceal his relationship with the actress Ellen Ternan. We recall too how George Eliot's cohabitation with a married man, George Henry Lewes, made her household a no-go area for her respectable contemporaries. In reacting against such rigidities, the public mind in the twentieth century has been pushed by the media further and further in the direction of moral anarchy. Yet Christians feel muzzled. So much suffering, as we have said, is caused by family breakdowns that only seemingly heartless prigs, we feel, could moralize about what has caused them when they occur.

If this is the case with marital breakdowns, how much more is it the case with homosexual practices? They have produced such appalling disasters for men and women since the onset of AIDS that pointing a finger at the personal responsibilities for the disasters will always be cruel in particular cases. No Christian would suggest that comforting the gravely afflicted ought to be diluted by pious recriminations. It is fitting that compassion should draw a veil over judgmental thinking. But pity for each and every individual case should not brim over into tacit acceptance of the practices that lie behind the physical breakdown.

This needs to be remembered because what the victims or their nearest and dearest say can sometimes so fill us with sympathy that we swallow an ethic of which we utterly disapprove. I will not name names, but I have read in the press a moving account of how a beautiful and gifted young woman of great promise as an artist was discovered to have AIDS and died at the age of twenty-nine. The press account tells us that she had never used needles and had "never been promiscuous." To corroborate the point the young lady's journal is quoted: "I have shared a bed with fewer men than I can count on both hands."

She was from a bohemian family and their environment was the art world. Such families perhaps adhered only lightly to social and moral convention. We may recall that the easing of moral constraints in the sexual field happened, for instance, in the Bloomsbury circle decades before it happened more widely. The liberated young men and women of the swinging sixties were in this respect the heirs of the writers and artists of the earlier decades.

The point to be made here is strictly a verbal one. And it is a matter of propaganda too. When readers have finished reading what is a moving piece in the press about a tragic loss, when they have been stirred to compassionate sympathy for a suffering household, have they not also been brainwashed into accepting the idea that premaritally sleeping with seven or eight or nine different men does not constitute "promiscuity" but rather represents a notable level of restraint, if not exactly chastity? The post-Christian mind does its work while feelings of sympathy and compassion are so stirred that it would be wickedly uncharitable to register exactly what is happening. After all, we have been told not to judge. And we have been told that the greatest of the virtues is charity. Thus compassion is sometimes a means of gently brainwashing us into connivance in the destruction of standards.

It is ironic that cultivation of the new codes against "discrimination" blurs the search for true equality. Equality between persons or groups, races or sexes, is not the same thing as similarity: still less is it the same thing as identicalness. There is much idle talk on this matter, especially in respect to the relationship between the sexes. I read in the press the complaint of a famous actress: "It's unfair that men don't have the problem of career versus children." Apparently she regrets the "unfairness" of the fact that men can concentrate single-mindedly on their careers while women have to experience the tug-of-war between the calls of motherhood and those of their chosen careers. Needless to say, she speaks with enthusiasm of her work on the stage. Clearly she loves it. But she also speaks dotingly of the delight her two little children bring her and how wonderful it is to be with them. Plainly she loves her time spent with them too.

In short, if one reads what she has to say with analytical care, her complaint is really that she has two different delights claiming her whereas a man could have only one. Now if a little girl complained that it was unfair for her brother to have two helpings of trifle while she had only one, this might reasonably win sympathy for her case. But if instead the little girl complained that whereas her brother had only a plate of trifle, she was compelled to switch her attention between a similar plate of trifle and a dish of ice cream, one might feel that her sense of logic was at fault. The actress certainly ought not to complain of unfairness when in fact she has two sources of delight where a man could only have one.

Thoroughly domesticated fathers may now protest that they do not recognize themselves in the role of the single-minded careerist blinded against the competing emotional demands of toddlers, but the interviewing journalist no doubt wanted to make a controversial point vividly. And it exemplifies the sad thinking that feminism has popularized.

At the back of it is a curious search for "equality." The notion that spreading equality among people is a matter of ridding the human world of differences that distinguish group from group, race from race and sex from sex is absurd. It is equally absurd to assume that such differences, while being tacitly recognized, ought somehow to be officially regarded as nonexistent. But the post-Christian mind is obsessed with ironing out the rich multiplicity of life. This is evident in the attempt to homogenize the sexes.

I have just read that a boxing match has taken place between two teenage girls in a Midlands city. It was planned a year ago but had to be called off because, when the event was publicly announced, there was a vast volume of protest against it. This time the organizers got their way by eschewing advance publicity. The event was staged at a Working Men's Club before a crowd of three hundred. The contestants were a girl of fourteen and one of thirteen, and the elder girl won by unanimous decision after three rounds. It seems extraordinary that this event should have been allowed when the British Medical Association had warned of the dangers of boxing at so young an age. Apparently the risks of damage to the eyes and to the brain are considerable. Common sense tells us that this is not a proper role for girlhood, that such exploitation of the aggressive instinct in active combat seems to make nonsense of every ideal of the feminine that our civilization has produced. But elimination of distinctions between the sexes has become an obsession in the post-Christian mind. It has affected enrollment in the armed services, in the police forces and in fire brigades. Up to a point it will work, partly because there are masculine women in the world just as there are feminine men, and partly because there are roles and functions peculiarly fitted to be performed by women in the work of these services. But there is evidence all around us of the costliness of pushing these homogenizing experiments too far. Day after day we read of cases of damages claimed by women for sexual harassment and for unjust discriminatory practices. We have not improved the relationships between the sexes by pretending that male and female are more or less the same anyway, and that the slight differences due to their distinctive roles in the perpetuation of the race are marginal to most central daily preoccupations. They are not marginal; they are central. It may have been "unfair" of the Almighty to give to womanhood its peculiar role in the reproductive process, but that's what he did. Yes, in his omnipotence he might have so arranged it that male human beings conceived and bore babies in the "odd" years while female human beings conceived and bore them in the "even" years. The physical machinery that would make possible such a sharing of pregnancy and birth between the sexes is not something we can imagine, let alone picture. But with God all things are possible, we are told.

What is the serious point behind the dialectical silliness? It is this: Christian men and women are taught to be grateful for God's creation of the world and its inhabitants. The desire to improve on the Creator's work is silly as well as arrogant. Accepting the pattern of the human family is generally a matter of joy as well as of obedience.

I sometimes wonder whether this same message is one that ought to be pressed on those who, in the name of "animal rights," are prepared to use violence against their fellow creatures. One cannot help feeling that, if the tenderness shown to animals by "animals rights" enthusiasts were generally shown to unborn babies, our civilization would not be disfigured as it is by the practice of abortion. The animal world is red in tooth and claw. The sleek tortoise-shell pussycat that drags its tail in seeming fondness against your legs or leaps onto your lap to be stroked is quite happy to go out into the garden afterward, seize a beautiful little bird and tear it to pieces. The beautiful little bird, with its bewitching twitches of the head and its endearing whistle, drags harmless worms out of the soil to destroy them in seeming savagery. As one who has never felt any inclination at all either to hunt foxes or to angle for trout, I still cannot understand how seemingly sensitive people can try to impose the morality of human relationships on the animal world and assume that all hunters and anglers are cruel monsters, their hands dripping with blood. This too is surely a question of discrimination. For it is a failure of true discrimination to try to iron out the discrepancies between human feelings and animal responses, as though basic differences between the human and animal order could be obliterated.

I have just read in a newspaper that "either you believe that an animal life is of equal value to a human one, or you don't: the modern sensibility decrees that it is." One may question what the word "value" means in this sentence. One may also question whether human "sensibility" is the faculty that arrives at judgments of this kind. But if the view cited here means that it is as wicked to tread on a worm as it is to smother a baby, then one must disagree. The hymn rightly praises God for the little bird that sings. But the same little bird gobbles up the worm. In animal lovers' eyes, was this arrangement a divine oversight? "Animal rights" enthusiasts need to be warned that it is dangerous to assume that here and there God failed as a Creator, and that it is their duty to try to correct these failings.

Another post-Christian device for obliterating crucial distinctions and thus undermining moral standards is the trick of associating what are really outrageous moral developments with the highbrow worlds of progressive literature and experimental art. We shall have cause to return to this link between corruption and artistic experiment later. Here, however, is an interesting instance of how the glamor of intellectual ability, like that of artistic status, can virtually light haloes around the heads of those whose tastes can corrupt the public. I turn to the weekly book pages of an important national daily. I find a full half-page devoted to a book by an academic called *A Defence of Masochism*. The book is indeed just that. According to the reviewer, the author of the book, a woman, makes some remarkable claims:

> Asserting that masochism is an intelligent, creative, misunderstood perversion which demonstrates "how psychologically healing sexual pain can be, in transforming inner trouble into something that your body can take and survive."

It appears that the author goes so far as to suggest that masochistic practices might aid in preserving the institution of marriage by spicing up jaded sexual palates. And under a large photograph of a human figure shrouded and tied up from head to foot there is the caption, "An argument that's bound to please: masochism made mainstream." Thus the caption frankly concedes the aim of decomposition implicit in so much post-Christian propaganda. For much of it is directed toward making all perversions and all peripherals "mainstream." This is an aspect of the relativization of concepts and values required by Aquarian mentalities.

One wonders whether the same Aquarian impulse is somehow behind the increasing demand for sex-change operations. For a man to want to be a woman or for a woman to want to be a man is a psychological situation so foreign to most of us that it is difficult to be fair to individuals so affected. If the change of sex were a matter of a simple corrective operation which solved the problem once and for all, it might seem to be no more a questioning of the created order than correcting a harelip and a cleft palate. But somehow the need to take hormonal treatment after a sex-change operation and for the rest of one's life seems to turn the whole procedure into a major and unwarranted interference with the natural order. If the new status cannot be sustained except by such drastic treatment, common sense suggests that it is an offense against nature. Yet the procedure seems to be increasingly regarded as unproblematic and acceptable. I find the following piece of news in the press.

> A copy editor at *The New York Times* graciously informed colleagues that he would soon be getting a sex-change operation. He went on to explain that he would be dressing as a woman in the coming months until the surgery is performed.

We know nothing more about the individual. How can we make moral judgments about this kind of thing? There may be cases where we can. Where the change is made by a husband

and father, one might suggest that consideration for the effect on his wife and children might have restrained him. But how can we judge the strength of his desire for womanhood? One question remains unanswered. Is it a mere coincidence that the demand for sex-change operations and the readiness to grant them has occurred at a time when the post-Christian mind is taking over in the media and in public opinion generally? Does the sense of dependence on a divine order for one's creation and preservation nurture obedient acceptance of one's individual gifts, including one's sexuality? And does the loss of that sense of dependence and gratitude lie behind the recent developments in the attitude to changes of sex?

Ten

The Body Beautiful

I f few of us find ourselves wishing we had been born into the opposite sex, many of us may wish from time to time that our bodies had been more handsomely constructed. And even if we are in youth fairly content with our personal appearance, we cannot live for long without sadly noting how it deteriorates. Poets throughout the ages have lamented the passage of youth into age, the loss of beauty and vigor and the eventual final parting with the body at death. Byron calls the body a "tenement of clay," a temporary dwelling for the human soul. Christian tradition treats the body as called to be the temple of the Holy Spirit. A proper respect for our own bodies is no doubt a duty. We must not damage them by dissipation or excess, or even by subjecting them to strains they are not designed to bear. This need for proper respect for the body is balanced in Christian teaching by the moral law against vanity.

I have just read of a shock received by a traveler making a train journey across Peru. At a village station he looked out of the carriage window on numbers of beggars and hawkers crowding up against the stationary train in the hope of either selling something to the passengers or begging for money. Among them was a man who limped along, begging for money and tapping his stick on the carriage windows to attract passengers' attention. He presented a feature from which the journalist involuntarily turned away in horror. It was the figure of a man with virtually no face. Where the face should have been, under a hat and shielded by a scarf, there was a moist-looking mess which a doctor among the passengers identified as a fatal cancerous growth.

This story reminds us of how blessed we are if we possess bodies not seriously damaged in any way. It also reminds us of how fortunate we are to live in societies where medical know-how is available to deal with the more unfortunate disfigurements that come people's way. Anyone acquainted with the treatment available these days for babies unfortunate enough to be born with a cleft palate and a harelip can testify to the great blessing that twentieth-century cosmetic surgery can bring. Earlier in our century, before cosmetic surgery was properly refined to deal adequately with this deformity, there were men and women walking the streets with grotesque faces and even more grotesque voices.

These thoughts come to mind as I read of some of the latest developments in cosmetic surgery. They seem to have been made, not in order to alleviate the sufferings of naturally disfigured men and women, but rather to satisfy the vanity of people who yearn for a more perfect physique or who refuse to accept what the passage of time does to every human body. The craze among women for having their breasts remolded by the use of silicone implants has not been of great benefit in many cases. I gather that a company which was once the biggest manufacturer of implants in the United States is on the verge of bankruptcy, for they are threatened with hundreds of demands for compensation from women who are suing them over side effects ranging from implant-rupture to rheumatoid arthritis.

One does not need to live very long to recognize that what

is a minority fashion in its early days may become a widely accepted one within a few years. For this reason it disturbs one to read about the latest developments in cosmetic surgery undertaken simply to beautify the face or the figure. Even though it is only the fairly wealthy few who can afford it at present, the temptations it presents may soon appeal to large numbers of women. I have been reading about a woman in her late forties who has spent thousands of dollars on cosmetic surgery. After a facelift, she chose to consult an ocular surgeon about further improvements. The treatment involved cutting away sections of her eyelids as well as dealing with crow's feet and eye bags. The new technique for this treatment involves use of a laser that vaporizes the human flesh. The laser can do what the scalpel cannot do. It can burn off tissue and seal the blood vessels. It can transform surface skin into white powder that can be brushed off. The after-effects are painful. The skin has been badly burned and has to be creamed and dressed accordingly. It takes weeks for the face to recover. And even then the patient is forbidden ever again to expose the affected skin to direct sunlight. Nevertheless, some months later, this lady is back in the hands of the cosmetic surgeon having a collagen injection in her lips to plump them out. When we read that the treatment in question involves obtaining tissue from human corpses, molding it and inserting it under the skin of the lips, we feel distinctly uncomfortable.

More uncomfortable, it would seem, than the lady herself or the partner she is anxious to please. The two of them are astrologers. She herself is influenced by the planet Venus and therefore has to make herself as attractive as possible. The lady's profession is that of psychic consultant who advises clients on personal matters such as love affairs or business concerns. She utilizes tarot cards and birth-chart readings.

Now, learning this, we become fully aware that we are, indeed, in the environment of the post-Christian era. We may have thought that here is a lesson for us on the dangers of giving way to the temptations of personal vanity. But the issue is a deeper one than that. No figure symbolizing vanity intrudes into the picture to lure the aging woman to seek desperately after lost beauty. We are not in the world under God, a world in which moral virtues and cardinal sins are locked in conflict for the possession of one more human soul. No, we are in a world governed by the gods and goddesses of the planets. Perhaps it is small wonder that the lady in question says, "I'm going to have the full face done next year."

The cult of the body beautiful is certainly not new. Nor is the obsession with sexual attractiveness which so often motivates it. In many ages there have been puritan moralists who have castigated contemporary sexual license, male predatoriness and female vanity. A lot is said today about the belief that we have escaped the excessive Victorian inhibitions and can be healthily frank in representing and appreciating the beauty of human beings in the natural state of nudity. Well, the good God designed our bodies, male and female. No healthy-minded Christian can regret that he devised the reproductive method that he did. Nevertheless, it is no accident that historically our genitalia have been called our "private" parts.

I remember, years ago, a lady reader writing in forceful protest to the editor of a women's journal that was making its first venture into pictorial representation of near-nudity. She did not say, "This is disgusting." She did not say, "I am outraged." She simply said, "Leave something for my bedroom." The point was a good one. In this sphere we have lost the distinction between the public and the private. It is just one more of those ironings-out of distinctions that mark the post-Christian age.

I have just read about a new magazine, *The Erotic Print Society Review*. It is described as "inventive" in the way it depicts human beings pleasuring themselves and others. Apparently one picture illustrates an episode from Petronius' *Satyricon,* in which a noblewoman uses the services of a priapic ass. In our simple-mindedness we may feel we are some distance away from today's much-advertised healthy reaction against Victorian prudery. Yet the editor, an Oxford graduate, assures us that she takes only what is of real artistic and literary quality, and that her journal stays above the dividing line that separates art from pornography.

The fact that the editor is a woman is perhaps a sign of the times. So too, perhaps, is the fact that she allows a large photograph of herself, smiling, to dominate the page in the press which publicizes her work. This strikes me with especial force because of another article in the very same newspaper on the very same day. I find it quite fascinating. It reveals how, earlier in our century, the London police prosecuted the editor of what was really a "lonely-hearts" magazine. Its purpose was to put lonely people in touch with others, which for the most part seems to have meant lonely women with men. It was called *The Link* and was subtitled "Monthly Social Medium for Lonely People." It had started in 1920, and was originally called *Cupid's Messenger.* No doubt the First World War had left many young and middle-aged women bereft and lonely. It is touching to see how the April 1921 issue shows young women repeatedly using the words "lonely," "very lonely" and "awfully lonely." Sometimes, of course, one smiles at the idiom of the age:

M. (London, E.C.). 25, educated, good-looking girl, is anxious to meet cultured, wholesome boy chum, 25-35, willing to escort her to dances. Good appearance necessary.

The police became involved partly because the journal did not confine itself to presenting the claims of lonely girls who wanted wholesome chums to take them to dances. Indeed, they found that the journal was being used too by homosexuals looking for contacts. Men were seeking "friendships" through its columns and were defining themselves as "broad-minded." The police answered some of the advertisements in false names to further their inquiries. As a result the editor was charged with printing and publishing advertisements to be used for "fornication" and the introduction of men to men for an unnatural purpose. The editor and three others were sentenced to two years of hard labor. The judge said there could be "no more grave attack on the morals of the country than to establish a paper for the purpose of allowing men and women to commit immorality." He regretted that the law did not allow him to impose penal servitude.

We smile at all this, most of us. And perhaps we might smile most at the fact that, presumably in the interests of propriety, the judge asked two women to withdraw from the jury because of the nature of the evidence. Should we be right to smile? I do not know. But the progress from being delicately asked to withdraw on account of one's feminine gender from hearing this case against *The Link* to editing and publicizing *The Erotic Print Society Review* marks a revolutionary change in the concept of womanhood effected by the post-Christian mind.

We have not yet finished with the subject of the body beautiful. I have just been reading a journalist's account of an interview with Marya Hornbacher, the American author of *Wasted*, a searing autobiographical record of her sufferings from bulimia and anorexia. In early childhood she decided that she was too fat. That was how her troubles started. In a desperate attempt to be thin she embarked on the now all-too-common progression through bulimia and anorexia, finishing up in a hospital time after time, but always renewing the mad craze until, at the age of eighteen and weighing less than sixty pounds, she almost died. This jolted her into a determination to live. But the damage already done to her heart, her muscles and her esophagus left her dependent upon regular monitoring of both body and mind. Marya Hornbach is now, not unnaturally, bitter in her criticism of the culture that brought her to this condition. She rails on the common obsession of women with slenderness and the consequent faddish preoccupation with diet and weight. And she knows where to put the blame. It is laid at the door of the fashion industry and the absurdity of the feminine physique it tries to popularize.

"Absurdity" is the right word because the slim, shapeless human clotheshorses on which fashion designers choose to hang their creations plainly do not represent any ideal of female beauty or attractiveness known to the human race. The Venus de Milo does not look as though she ever thought of weight-watching. In the living world the male preference for well-rounded women is well-attested. The skeleton, on the other hand, has in all ages been a distasteful object, the symbol of death. And the call that the walking skeletons of the fashion industry make to impressionable young girls is the call to suicide. It is as straightforward as that. Sometimes the call is fully answered. We have all heard of those tragic cases where young girls have slimmed themselves to death. Sometimes the call is seen through for all its bogusness, as it was by Marya Horn-bacher, but too late to allow her to live out a normal span in good health.

There is no need to underline here what is evident to all educated men and women, that the creations of the fashion industry are largely unwearable except on the catwalk. The object of their creators is always to astonish and very often to shock. Most of us laugh off the absurdities that decorate our journals on the fashion pages. The issue is so comical that it is scarcely worth getting excited about. Then suddenly we come across a case of a young life destroyed by the purveyors of this decadent non-sense, and we begin to wonder whether it is appropriate to laugh after all.

Even a distinguished actress has now turned her fire on these excesses. She argues in an article in *The Spectator* that many style gurus clearly "loathe women—not the anorexic, androgynous teenagers who stalk the catwalks like heroin addicts in search of a fix, but real women with real bodies." She cannot understand why women are prepared to be taken in by fashion gurus whose contempt for women is so glaringly obvious.

The excesses of the fashion world as displayed in our journals are matched by the excesses of the culinary world. Here is a slightly different indulgence of the body. It is not one which the victims of the cult for slimness are likely to be troubled by. Once again the excesses strike many of us as outrageous. Restaurants are recommended for their cuisine with a course-by-course record of what is available. The wine list is described. And then the price of the meal is quoted. And we are invited to leap mentally into a world where what is spent on one meal would keep a well-to-do family well fed for a week and, indeed, if the records of the charity appeals are to be believed, would plentifully sustain for longer than that a small village in one of the famine-stricken regions of Africa or Asia. We are, of course, commenting here on a level of indulgence that is open to a small minority of our total population. But it is clear from the pages of the glossy magazines that good eating and good drinking are a major preoccupation of a surprising number of middle-class households.

The purpose here is not to indulge a puritanical outburst against what is generally one of the most innocent delights of life. Rather it is to point to a contrast remarkable and inspiring. We have been looking at the worlds of *haute couture* and *haute cuisine*. And we marvel at the seeming excesses of indulgence in finery and food. Then we read, as I have just read, that the strictest of all religious orders in the Roman Catholic Church, the Carthusians, faces a crisis in England because of the increasing numbers of men wanting to join them. There is only one Carthusian monastery in the United Kingdom, but it can scarcely cope with the number of applicants for the novitiate. The regime is a very strict one, a pattern of silence, solitude, simplicity, prayer and denial. The monks eat, study, work and pray in their little cells, we are told. Three times a day they come out to join in worship in the chapel. Among those who have recently entered on this arduous life are a computer consultant, an air-traffic controller, a writer, an engineer and a musician. They do not sound like men whose lives in the world had nothing to offer them. Be that as it may, they represent an impressive Christian comment on the civilization we have built.

Their response to that civilization reminds us of the response of the desert fathers who fled from the world in the most decadent days of the later Roman Empire. By their flight to lives of prayer and study, simplicity and silence, austerity and discipline, these would-be monks compel us to ask ourselves the question: How decadent is our age? As the question arises I find an oddly relevant paragraph in the daily press. It is an outburst by an American feminist writer, Camille Paglia, against the decadence of the homosexual community.

> I'm getting sick and tired of the sentimental, feel-good, liberal propaganda that is concealing and denying the blatant, Nero-era decadence of so many gay men's lives, where compulsive, tunnel-vision promiscuity has become institutionalized.

Here the comparison with the decadence of Nero's Rome is expressly made. It underscores the attitude of the would-be Carthusian monks themselves. Greg Watts, a journalist who has written about them, quotes Fr. Cyril, the monk who deals with the applications to join the community.

> Fr. Cyril believes the traditional contemplative life, where silence speaks louder than words, has much to offer those searching for answers to the spiritual barrenness of the 1990s with its self-help books and New Age quackery. This search is likely to become more urgent as we approach the millennium.

Eleven

First Principles

We have all in our time, I suppose, been amused by the story of the Irishman who was asked, "Can you tell me the way to the railway station?" He replied, "Now if I was going to the railway station, I wouldn't start from here."

There is a devastating logic in this reply for which Christians frequently feel the need in the modern post-Christian world. When we are assailed with questions from the settled inhabitants of that world we all too often wish we could shift the ground. Someone perhaps asks us, "Do you think city brothels should be officially licensed and inspected?" We are rather nonplussed. We haven't given the matter much thought. We are inclined to distance ourselves from the issue. Should we perhaps reply flippantly, "I think it would be fairer to put the question to regular customers"? I have heard people similarly nonplussed by questioners on the radio. A media interviewer presses on some clergyman the question, "What do you as a Christian think we should do about famine in Indonesia?" or "What do you as a Christian think should be done about the genocide in Rwanda?" But the clergyman and Christians who happen to be listening to the interview cannot help reflecting that, if people were following Christian principles, there would be no famine in Indonesia and no genocide in Rwanda.

Here is a great gulf between the Christian and the post-Christian minds. Christians are taught to think in terms of fundamental first principles. We have the Ten Commandments as basic rules of conduct. The moral virtues have been defined for us and the deadly sins codified. But the post-Christian mind has divested itself of moral absolutes. It can be difficult, therefore, for us to reason with contemporaries who lack any such systematized sense of good and evil. Consequently, there is much discussion today that presupposes a kind of moral vacuum. There is also increasing inability to make reference to first principles. So far as moral and behavioral problems are concerned, the post-Christian mind operates on a level of derivation and subsidiarity. It bypasses the basic rational determinants of the situations it chooses to discuss.

Indeed, in order to clarify our thinking in this respect I have sometimes wondered whether it might be a good idea to ask the very theoretical question, "Suppose the world's entire population were converted to Christianity tomorrow, which of the major problems besetting humanity would prove at last soluble, and which major problems would remain insoluble?" For the purpose of clarifying our thinking, let us indulge this dream for a moment. Let us try to picture a world wholly inhabited by Christians. Let us assume that these converted people the world over put their Christian principles into practice to the best of their ability. And let us assume that their Christian governments direct things in such a way that there is nothing to impede any citizen from giving of his or her best. In that case, would it not follow that famine and abject poverty would be removed from the human scene? For surely the world's food production is potentially adequate to the needs of the human race. And surely if goods were distributed equitably and resources apportioned fairly, then there would no longer be vast discrepancies between the wealth and luxury of the favored few and the privations of the many who are deprived. Would not war too be abolished? For we are assuming that all people and governments would be striving for the betterment of conditions in their own countries and in other countries too. And we are assuming that there would be no wicked tyrants, no selfishly aggressive citizens, no government so corrupt that it could provoke rebellion. In that case there would be no issues for which to take up arms and no individuals ready to crush other individuals to death.

What is the point of dreaming up this ideal hypothesis? The world will never be like that, you will say. We Christians live in an imperfect world. Indeed, looking around on the national or international scene, we must confess that it is a very wicked and corrupt one. Strife and famine, oppression and injustice, flourish on a scale which makes a mockery of our dream. We are tempted to lend one ear to those who scoff at the notion that there can be a good God presiding over such evil and corruption. It is therefore necessary to remind ourselves that, in practical terms, Christianity would work in relation to the evils we have listed. A totally Christian population, wisely led, would be in a position to make life inconceivably better on our planet.

Two points follow from this deduction. One is that we can always reply without any qualms to the person who asks us, "How can you believe in a good God in the face of the mess that the world is in?" We can turn the question back on the questioner: "How can you expect the world to be other than in a mess when the good God and his laws are ignored?" The other point that emerges is this: Christians cannot possibly have at their fingertips immediate remedies for problems produced by behavior which they utterly deplore.

We have really posed two questions in one: In a world converted to Christianity, which major human problems would be soluble and which would prove insoluble? A totally Christian world would presumably be free of crime and free of the privations caused by selfishness. But it would certainly not be free of cancer and other diseases which can strike young lives with tragedy and misery. Cirrhosis of the liver caused by alcohol addiction would disappear from a world where individuals regarded their bodies as temples of the Holy Spirit. Cancer of the lung caused by tobacco would also disappear. Whatever diseases are caused by overindulgence, sexual promiscuity or addiction would be limited if not eliminated. But there would remain a mass of human suffering due to diseases and disabilities that no amount of human self-discipline could eradicate or even mitigate. No doubt, say, road accidents would be vastly reduced if every driver drove with due care and consideration, but there would remain a residue of what we call "pure accidents" in the world of machinery as well as natural disasters such as earthquakes, floods and tornadoes, which good intentions are powerless to avert. Moreover, the onset of old age, the season of strokes and senile dementia, would surely still cast a shadow over the lives of millions even in a morally and spiritually healthy world.

So when we are asked what is the Christian answer to this or that problem of privation or distress, we need to make a clear distinction between evils that result from human wickedness or folly, and ills such as natural disasters and the afflictions of mortality. There can scarcely be specifically "Christian" solutions to problems produced by anti-Christian behavior. Too often nowadays we hear questions discussed which are subsidiary to larger questions that are not explicitly aired. For instance, consider the question: Should capital punishment for murder be abolished? The force of the word "should" is clearly not the same as it would be in the question, "Should anyone murder a fellow being?" Plainly, the first question stands in subordinate relation to the second. Anyone who is acutely conscious of moral generalizations such as "No one should ever commit murder" may be uncomfortable with the weak relativity of the word "should" in "Should capital punishment be abolished?"

I have taken a rather stark and crude example of what I mean by questions of primary or subsidiary obligation. Only if a person has broken the moral law against murder could the question arise: "Should a murderer be executed or imprisoned?" And only if this second question had been settled could a question more subsidiary still arise, such as "Should convicted murderers serving life sentences be allowed conjugal visits?" This distinction between primary and subsidiary questions is increasingly relevant to controversies today. And because Christian thinking is always alert to unexamined premises, we cannot give our minds simplistically to derivative problems in isolation. Someone raises the question: Ought we to distribute free condoms to boys to protect them and others from AIDS? Someone else raises the question: Ought we to distribute contraceptive pills to young girls to protect them from unwanted pregnancies? The Christian mind is uncomfortable with this use of "ought." For such questions cannot be isolated in Christian thinking from the unexamined premise: The young are going to break the Christian moral law habitually in respect to sexual behavior.

It is in relation to the moral law against sexual activity outside marriage that the Christian is accustomed to use the word "ought," or rather the words "ought not."

There is a fine city in the United Kingdom which attracts tourists from all over the world to sample its historic splendors. But not long ago I read an article in the press about a rundown housing estate in the city, where families live in grinding poverty. Unemployment is the norm there, crime and delinquency are rife. Behind the visible squalor and decay there are familiar stories of broken homes, alcoholism and despair. What makes this picture of urban dereliction especially tragic is that addiction to heroin spread among the young men and women there during the 1980s. At first, in a well-meaning attempt to counter growing addiction, the local police imposed a clampdown on the sale of hypodermic syringes. Ten years later, of course, the police would have known better than to adopt that policy, but it was before the AIDS scare had spread. As it was, in consequence of this restriction, addicts took to the habit of sharing needles. The sharing resulted in a rapid spread of the HIV virus among the addicts. Oddly enough, the addicts were on the whole hostile to homosexuality. And they were not markedly promiscuous. But transmission of the virus through normal sexual partnerships proved devastating. There were stories of young men and women whose first experience of coition left them infected.

Could the police be blamed for the fact that hypodermic needles were difficult to obtain? They acted for the best with their knowledge at the time. When eventually the cry arose, "Needles should be made freely available," the advice was followed. Here we have a very subsidiary "moral" question indeed. "*Should* hypodermic needles be made freely available to drug addicts in view of the way AIDS is being spread?" There is not much moral universality about the "should" in that question. It is a very different "should" from that in the questions "Should young people have sex indiscriminately outside marriage?" or "Should young people become dependent on heroin?" If we are to get involved in controversy with our contemporaries, the sense of moral obligation connoted by the various usages of the word "should" needs to be clarified. The degree of moral obligation needs to be measured. This has to be said because the post-Christian mind has become obsessed with sometimes specious "obligations" which arise only because fundamental obligations have been ignored.

Our society has become genuinely more compassionate. And no Christian ought to pretend that there can be any excuse for failing to respond to need and to suffering when and where they occur. We are not told that the good Samaritan made any inquiries as to whether the injured traveler he aided might have brought his troubles upon himself. But the post-Christian world occupies itself feverishly (and properly) with trying to undo damage caused by situations which ought never to have been allowed to develop in the first place.

I am aware that, at this point in the argument, readers may protest that I am urging a callous weighing of deserts to precede compassionate action. But I am not. For I am not writing a book about healing the world's suffering. I am writing a book about correcting slovenly thinking. Above all, I am writing a book about the need to get behind the subsidiary practical moral questions of the day to the primary moral imperatives which we have neglected at devastating cost.

Here it should be said in parentheses that there are, of course, social as well as moral implications in the existence of an area of poverty in an otherwise fine historic city. Another primary moral imperative hangs in the back of the mind, and it leaves us with an awkward question. *Should* there be an area of grinding poverty, mass unemployment and urban dereliction within a city whose finer areas have abundance of wealth and draw tourists to their attractions from all over the world?

That, however, is not the main issue at this point. I am concerned with the fact that the post-Christian mental environment is alive with problems and controversies which we Christians must necessarily feel have been artificially created, indeed almost intentionally created. Should homosexual partners be granted the same legal status as married couples? A lesbian couple have just taken to the European Court their complaint that a railway company employing one of them refused to grant her partner the special allowances for inexpensive travel and other perquisites normally allowed to an employee's spouse. Ought we to get excited about this subsidiary issue? For it arises simply because great primary Christian imperatives are being treated as belonging to the past.

We come across comparable subsidiary problems when people agitate for the rights of single parents. Now, of course, there are single parents and single parents. There are married women whose husbands have left them. There are single mothers whose partners have deceived and abandoned them. But there are also lots of lone parents who have chosen single motherhood. They form part of a vocal body now so numerous that they constitute a political lobby whose demands have to be listened to. And, indeed, their claims have to be responded to with charity and understanding. No genuine Christian could doubt that. But, likewise, no genuine Christian can listen to the complaints case by case without silently asking the question, "Well, why did you become a single mother anyway?"

It has become indecent to utter any such question aloud. A new post-Christian etiquette is being imposed on the public. They are not allowed to inquire, "Why did you?" or "How did it come about?" in reference to any offspring born from among the vast concourse of single mothers who solicit our sympathy and the support of the state. Just as Victorian children were not allowed to ask where babies came from, just as it was the custom to speak in the presence of the young as though babies fell from a tree in the garden or were dropped down the chimney by a flying stork, so nowadays a great pretense has to be preserved that all single motherhood results from accidents on a par with losing one's passport or afflictions equivalent to a common cold. The sheer hypocrisy of the present conspiracy against plain speaking is breathtaking.

We have already noticed how, by use of the expression "marriage breakdown," the post-Christian mind has begun to treat divorce as a misfortune to which married couples have contributed nothing in the way of responsibility. The post-Christian mind has invented the "no-fault" divorce for which the entire responsibility can be laid on a marriage which, when taken home and tried out, proves to be faulty. The post-Christian mind is now getting us accustomed to the notion of a "no-fault" pregnancy which descends on its victims unaccountably like influenza or chicken pox.

Christians must be realistic. We must know the world we live in. We must give our attention as carefully as anyone to the practical problems that touch the lives of others with misery and despair. But mentally we must never lose our grasp of the great moral universals that our faith prescribes as principles of conduct. And we must not hesitate in discussion to shift the ground of argument from what is subsidiary to what is primary in prescriptions for human behavior.

Twelve

Democracy

In the last decades of our century government by democracy has been adopted by more and more countries. Eastern European nations, after long subjection to Marxist totalitarianism, have proudly proclaimed their conversion to democracy. Leaders of the Soviet Union have found that they could satisfy the clamor of their populations only by embracing policies of democratization. It is obvious that totalitarian systems destroy freedom and stifle initiative. "Democracy" means government by the people, that is, government under which sovereign power resides, not in any individual, any family or any specially privileged class, but in the hands of the national community as a whole.

History has proved that democracy alone can safeguard peoples from tyranny and injustice. The principle is so self-evident to us that many of us have come to assume that it is of valid application to all or most areas of social life. If a nation can be ruled best by an elective system in which the voices of all have equal weight through the ballot box, does it not follow that any institution or society will be most healthily directed by a similar system? Indeed, we happily transfer the electoral system to our professional associations and to other such societies, choosing committees of management by giving all members the right to vote. The advantages of using electoral systems are evident. To try to defend a less open or more authoritarian way of running an institution would seem absurd. An ironic citizen in nineteenth-century Czarist Russia is reputed to have said, "Every country has its own constitution; ours is absolutism moderated by assassination."

Why do we need to look more closely at something so evidently valuable as the principle of democracy? Because by an easy but illogical sequence of thought it may be assumed that, because we are all equal and share the right to partake in electing our rulers, anyone's opinion on any matter is as valid as anyone else's. Plainly this is not the case. Taking a majority vote may be the safest system of electing people to govern us. But it does not follow that taking a majority vote would be the best method of arriving at the truth in any area of practical or theoretical discussion.

What is the philosophical or moral principle behind attachment to democracy? I have seen it argued that the right of every man and woman to be consulted over the choice of who shall govern them is especially dear to Christians because they accept that all men and women are equal in the sight of God. But how far does this equality extend? Is the general understanding of the complex issues of modern civilized life such that every man and woman in the street is equally qualified to judge the best way to grapple with them or the best people to tackle them? We cannot pretend that it is so. Indeed, George Bernard Shaw very perceptively observed that "democracy substitutes election by the incompetent many for appointment by the corrupt few." This observation, comic as it is, actually gets to the heart of the matter. The many who vote may or may not be, for the most part, "incompetent," but what is the alternative to giving them their say? The alternative is rule by the "corrupt few."

In other words, democracy is necessary because of what it protects us from. "All power corrupts and absolute power corrupts absolutely." The practice of democracy safeguards us from corruption and tyranny because it enables us to get rid of governors who would be corrupted by the unfettered exercise of power. Thus the principle of democracy does not in itself testify that everyone is so competent that their opinion must be acted upon. The principle of democracy testifies that everyone is so subject to corruption that the reins of power must not be left for long in anyone's hands without check. The basis of the democratic principle is the Christian doctrine of original sin. We are all corruptible. Holding power and exercising authority over others is potentially an especially corrupting position. The less power gets into the hands of any individual on a permanent basis, the better. So, Christians do not get enthusiastic about democracy because all men and women are blessed with good judgment; Christians get enthusiastic about democracy because they know that all men and women are subject to temptation and corruption.

The virtues of democracy are negative. And that is why we must be wary of extending the principle into areas of life other than the political. Even in the sphere of government democracy can fail to be effective. The popular vote may put a vicious dictator into power. In these days, when the mass media are so powerful in brainwashing the public, the votes of the masses may be manipulated by wielders of wealth and power. To assume that the masses always know best is folly.

What has all this got to do with the analysis of the post-Christian mind and the exploration of where it collides with genuine Christian thinking? To explain this let me say that so-called "democratic" notions of how people should function in, for instance, education have done great damage in recent decades. By an easy, but false, transference of thought, it is possible to move from the principle that all human beings are equal to the notion that anybody's opinion is as good as everybody else's, and that the exercise of authority by parents over children and teachers over pupils needs to be curtailed. But education is a means of handing on knowledge and skills from generation to generation. We might cite as examples the processes of learning to speak or learning to calculate. For in these matters the individual is endowed with understanding only by submission. We can learn to speak, to think and to read only through acquaintance with the language of our race. And language is not an individual possession. It is a traditional inheritance handed down from generation to generation. And it works because of the authority that it enshrines, an authority sustained by universal submission to it. It is because we all agree to accept what the word "good" means and what the word "bad" means that we can reason and judge. And it is because we accept regulations about word order that we can distinguish in meaning between, for example, "Children must obey their parents" and "Parents must obey their children" and communicate sensibly with one another.

There can be no education without submission to disciplines. The people who benefit most from education are those who have submitted themselves most rigorously to the disciplines involved in learning languages, in acquiring mathematical skill and scientific expertise, in mastering a keyboard. Children can astonish us by their eagerness to learn, by their readiness to apply themselves and by the freshness of the thoughts they sometimes express. In consequence a trend grew in educational circles of treating children as though their "creative" capacity was all-important. The growing idea that individuality had its own source of creativity within made the practice of submitting children to disciplines inappropriate. We do not need to ponder the celebrated accounts of children brought up by wolves in order to understand that individuality can be harnessed to fruitful purpose only within the frameworks of society, only under the disciplines of dictionary and grammar, of code and regulation. Human beings cannot become sources of inventiveness* unless their individuality has been overlaid by the intellectual endowments which civilization is prepared to hand on to them if they cooperate with its formulations.

I read today of an annual conference of teachers at which parents are being criticized for assuming that their children are always in the right, even when teachers have disciplined them for their faults. One delegate complained that "parents give their children everything they want and don't tell them off." Another delegate told how a parent had stormed into a classroom and physically assaulted a teacher after the teacher had rebuked his child for a misdemeanor. What is interesting to the objective observer of these developments is that the generation of parents thus under fire is, of course, the generation who as children were brought up in schools during the worst phase of the "child-centered" classroom approach which was so weak

---

* I recall that once, as a student, I used the word "creative" in one of my essays in reference to a writer. My tutor, C.S. Lewis, said, "You mean 'inventive.' Only God can be 'creative.'"

on discipline. It is surely the trendy educationalist of the sixties and seventies whose work we are now in a position to judge.

Biblical imagery could perhaps help us to clear our minds on this matter. Most of us can probably recall sermons about the Good Shepherd. We have all been reminded from time to time by earnest preachers how the Jewish shepherds worked. The Jewish shepherd led his sheep from the front and had such knowledge of individual sheep that he could call them all by their names. This is necessary information for a congregation living in a sheep-rearing area, as I happen to do. No shepherd here could get his sheep to follow him anywhere. He drives them from behind. Or rather his sheep dogs drive them, responding with seemingly miraculous understanding to the instructions he conveys by whistling. Does he know the sheep individually? Not by name, I think. Yesterday I saw a crowd of newborn lambs in a field, all neatly numbered on their sides in blue paint. There is something incongruous about a white lamb with "47" in large figures painted on its side. But no doubt the number represents the first step in guaranteeing a correct relationship between parent and offspring.

Be that as it may, I have introduced this topic because the biblical use of the sheep and shepherd imagery seems to recommend an attitude of meek obedience to authority. And St. Peter, in his first epistle, declares, "For ye were as sheep going astray; but are now returned unto the Shepherd and Bishop of your souls" (1 Pt 2:25). So the King James Bible has it, translating the guardianship of sheep into the idiom of ecclesiastical organization. This symbolic connection has always been evident in the use of the Latin word for "shepherd," *pastor*, and the corresponding adjective *pastoral* for the work of the Christian ministry.

Shepherds without sheep would have no raison d'être. And shepherds who did not guide, nurture and care for their sheep would scarcely fulfill their proper roles. What has always worried me in the back of my mind is the sharp antithesis between the notions here—of the shepherd's role and the sheep's acquiescence—and notions of "democratic" relationships so much recommended by the post-Christian mind. Our Lord said to Peter, "Feed my lambs" and "Feed my sheep." And plainly he was not just thinking of the supply of food and water. He must have been thinking of nourishment of the mind and the soul. "Feed my sheep." That is what our Lord said. He did not say, "Engage my sheep in fruitful dialogue. Get them all to share their personal opinions. Persuade each and every one of them to make their individual contributions so that together they can arrive at the truth. And above all induce them to think creatively and not to accept anything for gospel just because you say it."

"Preach the gospel!" Such instructions imply the existence of people prepared to listen, prepared to learn and prepared to obey. It all sounds more like the motto for a Victorian school classroom than for a modern seminar. The basic principle of "democracy" remains much the safest and healthiest system of government that history has produced. But the post-Christian notion that so-called democratic methods of approach and procedure are equally applicable to all spheres of human action and human development is absurd. In the Christian life we are not all shepherds. If we were, there would be no sheep. And acting as shepherds without any sheep is a peculiarly useless vocation.

We may well ask, however, who are the shepherds of today's unchurched flocks? To whom do they look for inspiration and guidance? This matters especially in respect to the young. What sort of models are being put before the young? I read today of a popular TV presenter of a chat show being mobbed by girl students at one of our better universities. The adulation may be justified on the grounds of his personal charm, his wit and his deftness in repartee. Well and good. But the journalist reporting with admiration on his qualities had this to say:

> Since his marriage there have been "relationships that have come and gone." Now he has what he calls "an association" with X [a radio presenter and actress]. "I like a reasonably structured way of living. I want my own space but I wouldn't rule out further commitment."
>
> In May 1987 he unexpectedly became a father from an on-again-off-again relationship with the journalist and broadcaster Y. "We had a relationship, lost touch and then got back together. She's a very likeable and competent girl. But there was no question of our marrying or living together."

Is it an exaggeration to say that the TV presenter and the journalist are involved together in one more move to decompose our moral sense? So polite are we that no one who happens to have inherited the traditional moral codes of Christendom is going to call a spade a spade in this connection. And what counterforce against this moral anarchy is going to weigh upon the student mind or the public mind generally? Have the students been brought up by parents who would correct any tendency to swallow the cheap values of the media stars? Are they all regular churchgoers who will listen on Sundays to pious outbursts against moral laxity that might lead them to question the way of life encouraged by the media? It is very unlikely.

Is it surprising then to read that the shape of family life in Britain has been altered radically within the span of a generation? More than one child in five now grows up without two parents in the home. In 1971 just 8 percent of families with children had a lone parent. The latest figure is 22 percent. Neither the TV presenter nor the journalist who presents the presenter is helping much in this respect.

Where, indeed, is the voice of moral sanity? If we seek it in the media, we are unlikely to find it. Here is an excerpt from a reader's contribution to a magazine on the subject of adultery:

> Adultery isn't particularly desirable, but nor is it a sin.... It's difficult to be monogamous. You fall in love with someone and don't look at anyone else, but the years pass, and things change. I've never been married long enough to know how long monogamy is realistic. I imagine about seven years. [The writer is a woman of eighty-five.]

One wonders what the word "sin" means to this writer. My latest dictionary defines it as "transgression of God's known will or any principle or law regarded as embodying this." Insofar as there is any formulation generally accepted in Western civilization as embodying divine law, it surely must be the Ten Commandments, one of which specifically condemns adultery. Linguistically speaking, the lady would have a perfect right to say, "Adultery is sinful in the eyes of Christians, but I don't agree with that."

It is curious that another contributor to the same topic, who otherwise writes sensibly and firmly against adultery, nevertheless finishes like this: "Adultery is a crying shame, and the children suffer. I see it not so much as sinful, but morally incorrect."

It seems clear that the concept of "sin" is being lost to the post-Christian mind. The concept of "moral correctness," whatever it may mean, presumably has the advantage of eliminating any notion of obligation to divine authority.

A grave question arises from all this. Suppose our children were being taught daily in Christian schools by Christian teachers, would that influence be strong enough to counteract the pervasive decomposition of morality and logic that issues from the popular media? The appalling "authority" which the media obtain by sheer theft over the minds of the young is a poisonous stain on our civilization. False idols and false gods are fashioned in the increasingly worthless worlds of pop and rock, and cheap entertainment. One might think this language extravagant, were it not that voices from within that world confirm it. I have just read a journalist's account of an interview with Sean Lennon, the son of John Lennon. There is no need to repeat the disparaging terms he uses about the character of the famous Beatle. What is interesting is the seeming necessity for the son to confute the idolators of his father.

People forget how easy it is to overglorify a human being, to make a myth of them....

I don't want people to think I'm being disrespectful. But then again, he's my dad, and I know better than they do. I know he was a great guy, but he wasn't a god, he was a person like you and me. He was imperfect....

Are there really masses of people out there who need to have their ideas corrected thus? Have we freed our populations from undemocratic subservience to aristocrats and tyrants only to see them fall down on their faces in idolatry before the amoral gods of the modern media?

Thirteen

Freedom

No value is dearer to the democratic Western mind than "freedom." No one today wants to be accused of limiting other people's freedom. Yet the post-Christian mind has contrived so to twist the meaning of words that people find it possible to accuse Christians of offenses against individual freedom when freedom is exercised, to say prayers in schools, for instance. What was established in the Constitution of the United States as a guarantee against government regulation of religious creed and worship has been twisted into a means of imposing an anti-Christian tyranny on believers. In tackling this problem we have the advantage of a firm biblical account of what freedom is, and it comes from the mouth of our Lord himself. "Then said Jesus to those Jews which believed on him, If ye continue in my word, then are ye my disciples indeed; And ye shall know the truth, and the truth shall make you free" (Jn 8:31-32). The peculiar interest of this definition is that Jesus was immediately tackled over what he meant: "What are you talking about? We are all Abraham's descendants and not in bondage to anyone." But Jesus pressed his definition home with great precision. "Verily, verily I say unto you, Whosoever committeth sin is the servant of sin" (Jn 8:34).

The word "servant" here means "slave." The slave is not a

free member of a household. He lives in bondage there.

There is surely here a stark contradiction between our Lord's definition and the popular conception today of what it means to be free. You get to a junction in the road and you are free to turn left or right. A man or a woman is free to marry or to stay single. Every citizen is free to vote for a right-wing candidate or for a left-wing candidate. What this amounts to is that we locate freedom in the empty space before a decision is made. But Christ's words seem to locate true freedom in the space that follows upon decision. You may choose to sin or not to sin, but if you choose to sin you have lost your freedom and have become a slave to sin. Freedom appears to be something that you gain or forfeit. It seems to stand on the further side of choice and decision.

In contemporary usage the words "He has gained his freedom" might be said of a man who had just been let out of jail after serving a sentence. The state of "freedom" here is characterized by the removal of restraints, the seeming restoration of choice in respect to where the released convict goes or lives. But, of course, we all know, in the back of our minds, that if John Smith has just finished ten years of penal servitude and leaves the prison gates behind him without a job or a home to go to, or enough money in his pocket to feed and clothe and house himself for more than a week, then his "freedom" assumes the character of a technicality rather than a living reality. We can even imagine such a man saying to himself, "I felt freer inside," in that the pressures that now accompany the search for food and shelter and employment were not pressing upon him in the cell or the exercise yard.

Ironically enough, in contemporary post-Christian usage the

words "He has gained his freedom" might just as easily be said of a man who had just been granted a divorce from his wife. This usage is interesting. It seems to imply that the married person is shackled in some way. But marriage is a state into which couples enter freely. In so doing they make vows of fidelity. It is difficult to think of any other situation where the breaking of promises freely and solemnly made could be equated even in the post-Christian mind with an escape into freedom. If a member of a golf club failed to pay the annual subscription which he voluntarily pledged to pay, or if he persistently broke the club's regulations which he voluntarily pledged to accept, the club authorities might well dispossess him of his membership. A player so dispossessed might find comfort in some perverse reasoning, but he could scarcely claim thereby to have "gained his freedom."

One of the most oft-quoted statements about freedom is that made by the seventeenth-century English poet Richard Lovelace. Lovelace was a wealthy and courtly Cavalier who served King Charles I in his struggle with Parliament. He was imprisoned for a time in 1642, and this imprisonment was the price he paid for being involved in presenting a petition to Parliament for the retention of the *Book of Common Prayer* and of episcopacy, which the Puritan Parliament made illegal. Thus Lovelace was very much a prisoner of conscience and he wrote the celebrated poem "To Althea" from his prison cell. It contains a remarkable stanza.

> Stone walls do not a prison make,
> Nor iron bars a cage;
> Minds innocent and quiet take
> That for an hermitage.

If I have freedom in my love
And in my soul am free,
Angels alone, that soar above,
Enjoy such liberty.

That is all very well, one may say. The thoughts are fine. And perhaps, with a stupendous effort, we can persuade ourselves that some great souls may rise above their circumstances and strive to defeat their enemies' intentions by assuring them that they feel inwardly free even in a prison cell. But poetry is not the same thing as real life. And sentiments of this kind might sound very hollow in the ears of a hostage spending his third year in the hands of terrorists. Nevertheless, it must be accepted that there is something about the human spirit that can transcend the limitations of imprisonment. The determination of a tyrant to enslave another person may produce in the Christian victim a determination not to feel enslaved, not to submit his will to his captors.

As long as we define freedom simply in terms of the absence of constraints, we fail to allow for the state of mind that produced Lovelace's poem and has produced many noble instances in our own century of refusal to bend the will and surrender the spirit in the face of all that persecution could do. Heroic survivors of Nazi brutalities in World War II, and heroic martyrs to those brutalities too, were men and women who refused to surrender their inner freedom of mind and heart in the face of vicious attacks on their external freedom.

A man held under the maximum physical constraint, then, may preserve something that we call his inner freedom—freedom of mind and spirit. What about the man who is subject to the very opposite experience? Suppose a man wins a fortune on a lottery that turns him overnight into a millionaire. Constraints that have fettered him all his life are suddenly removed. Is not this the essence of "freedom"—to be liberated from the need to earn your living by daily employment, from the need to dig your own garden, clean your own house and make your own meals? All constraints upon expenditure are suddenly lifted. The lucky person is "free" to spend money on clothes, entertainment, food and drink, travel and all the tempting accessories of daily life. Yet when individual cases of such sudden good fortune are investigated by the media, it emerges that the experience nearly always turns sour. Sometimes it is a simple case of overindulgence that leads to alcoholism or some other addiction. Sometimes the access to wealth destroys previously harmonious relationships between man and wife, parents and children, brothers and sisters.

Those who have experienced these calamities would not claim that money had in fact replaced a state of servitude with a state of freedom. On the contrary, their daily pattern of work in their earlier days, with its rhythm of toil and rest, application and recreation, is something they look back on with regret for its loss. By the sudden access of wealth, money "took over" their lives. It emerges that the constraints of the ordered working life can give a sense of well-being that is utterly destroyed when all those constraints are removed. Money, which is expected to free people, can take over their lives and enslave them.

The notion that freedom essentially consists in the absence of constraints will not hold water. Indeed, constraints are often a guarantee of freedom. It is because our country's laws do not leave us "free" to choose which side of the road to drive on that we can freely move about. A series of constraints has been formulated to guarantee our freedom in that respect. There are rules about yielding at crossroads, about pausing at traffic lights, about when to dim the headlights. If someone suggested to you that these regulations constituted a tyrannous diminution of your freedom, you would reply, "On the contrary, it is because these regulations are enforced that we can freely drive about our roads in safety." The constraints provide an essential safeguard of our freedom as drivers. Without them roads on which streams of traffic now move smoothly and safely would be clogged up quickly with crashed vehicles.

Far from reducing freedom, constraints and regulations may confer freedom. This, of course, is one of the principles on which our civilization has been built. It was the principle behind laws and protocols accepted in the past, even those that condemned witchcraft, adultery and homosexual practices. No doubt we are right to have escaped such legislation. But we need to recall that the more recent abolition of restraints that protected marriage and the family can scarcely be said to have been productive of greater happiness, increased mental stability or reduced crime.

It is ironic that the notion of democratic freedom should have been interpreted in such a way that true freedom in religious matters is imperiled. The official grant of religious freedom for all in the United States has been turned on its head. Because no religious body has the right to claim official status under the government, modern so-called liberal opinion operates toward denying freedom of expression in public to Christian bodies. As a result there is controversy about forbidding prayer in state schools or the use of Christian symbols in official buildings. There is a wise proverbial piece of advice about the absurdity of sawing off the branch of a tree on which you happen to be sitting. In the once-Christian West this practice is now common in arguments against demonstrations of Christian allegiance. The post-Christian mind is quite prepared to inherit the traditions of Christian practice while emptying those practices of Christian content. A good example, of course, is the increasing celebration of Christmas as an occasion for parties and present-giving, and an encouragement to all manner of indulgence. For as the retail and holiday industries make more and more of the annual festival, the Christian basis is increasingly ignored. One even receives supposed "Christmas" cards from which the very word "Christmas" is banned. The card does not wish us "A Merry Christmas." Instead the sender presents the recipients with "the compliments of the season" or some other such anodyne message.

I find in my newspaper today an astonishing instance of how Christian occasions can be taken over and their Christian essence denied. Tomorrow is St. Patrick's Day, the seventeenth of March. St. Patrick is the patron saint of Ireland. There will be a massive parade in Dublin. But the organizers ban religious and political groups from taking part in the official parade. As a result, a Roman Catholic body, the Our Lady of the Rosary National Crusade, has been refused permission to take part. They wanted to parade with crosses, rosaries and religious statues. To make matters worse, it so happens that the theme of this year's parade is to be magic and wizardry. A spokeswoman for the Catholic organization is quite outraged. "The parade is full of the pagan symbols of snakes, wizards and warlocks that St. Patrick came to Ireland to get rid of. The work of the devil is going and we have to stop it."

Whether this is making too much of the seeming affront I do not know. What interests me, and what is perhaps most significant of all, is the response of the parade's executive director. "The whole parade is a celebration of Christianity. I cannot think of anything more spiritual than expressing yourself through art." This is the post-Christian mind with a vengeance. "Nothing more spiritual" than expressing yourself through art. *Nothing?* Not saying your prayers? Not going to worship in church? Not reading your Bible? Not meditating in quiet? This indeed is a fine specimen of the linguistic takeover that we witness so often. What does the director's statement really amount to? It amounts to this: We are preventing this Catholic organization from taking part because we are the real genuine celebrators of Christianity, the real guardians of the spiritual life. We are really more Christian than the Christians. Indeed. Aslan is Tash. Tash is Aslan.

The reason why the post-Christian mind just cannot put up with Christianity deserves to be clarified. The claim of Christianity is that it holds universal truth to which, in the long run, all particular, all lesser knowledge will prove to have a subsidiary, contributory status. This claim is unacceptable in the world of the media, which is imbued with post-Christian presuppositions. The claim of Christianity is that it is rooted in an eternal order overarching the limited events that take place within finitude. The post-Christian mind cannot bear such pretensions. But it does not therefore find it convenient to try to dispose directly of Christianity. The post-Christian mind is determined rather to recategorize Christianity, to shift it bodily from its transcendent moorings and to site it alongside systems of opinion untainted by authoritative supernaturalism. Situated thus, it sits alongside agendas that happily allow themselves to be over-arched by the one real contemporary imperative which is presented as "freedom of thought." And, as now exploited, the expression "freedom of thought" is just another form of words to define total absence of conviction. The words are the *Open Sesame* to the Aquarian realm of conceptual fluidity. "Freedom of thought," as now accepted, is in effect an ultimate commitment to nonthought.

Current post-Christian verbal usage tends to locate "freedom" in a vacuum, in a state of mental openness to various options prior to commitment to any of them. The Christian concept of "freedom" is of an endowment granted on the further side of commitment. It does not occupy an empty space before anything has happened: it is a blessing purchased after a ransom has been paid.

Fourteen

Freedom of Expression

There is no topic more taxing to the mind than that of censorship. It has now become generally accepted that to limit freedom of expression is dangerous. The post-Christian mind claims to loathe censorship by law. But there is one exception to this distaste. It is agreed that the law should offer protection from insult to minority ethnic groups. This protection is accepted by the post-Christian mind because it can pose as something other than censorship even though it actually functions as censorship.

The avowed object is to make "incitement to racial hatred" a punishable offense. That is acceptable to the post-Christian mind because the emphasis of attention is shifted from the question "Is this published material in itself evil, tasteless or repellent?" to the question "Will this published material be hurtful or damaging to any minority ethnic group in the population?" We have seen already that the post-Christian mind is always happy to replace the codes of traditional personal morality by criteria of social damage-limitation. Hence the readiness to be tender of offending vulnerable groups. This emphasis then becomes effective in respect to forms of expression other than those concerned with matters of relationship between the races or the sexes or other groupings. Thus when moralists protest against the representation of gross obscenities in literature or on television, the reply tends to stress that the adult public have the freedom to close their magazines or turn off their screens. The only issue allowed to be considered is whether the material is presented in such a way or at such a time that it is highly likely to be observed by children.

Children apart, debates about what is to be allowed or forbidden on the TV screen or on the printed page tend to revolve around the notion of "offensiveness." Obscene programs on the screen are defended on the grounds that "very few people are offended by them." So far as such displays of obscenity are concerned, whether of prurience or violence, there is a suspicion at the back of my mind that the only people who are not damaged by what they see may be those very people who in fact really are "offended." What is important, surely, is the damage done to those who are not offended, who take the obscene display for granted, assimilate it as naturally as the primmest old maiden lady might assimilate a play based on Mrs. Gaskell's *Cranford*. In this respect I suppose the issue of freedom of expression in relation to sex or violence is slightly different from that of freedom of expression in relation to matters that are sacred or venerable in the eyes of large sections of the population.

The issue of censorship is confused by the fact that great defenders of the freedom of the press in the past, like John Milton for instance, were concerned to resist the suppression of dissent by tyrannical governments. This historical fact lends to those who defend every kind of freedom of expression a seeming streak of nobility which disarms criticism. But what are the facts which face both the enemies and the advocates of censorship today? An unfortunate, unbalanced young man watches on the television screen a dramatic episode in which a woman is raped and then strangled. So disturbed is he that he goes out to find a victim to whom he can give the same treatment. When we are faced with events like these, common sense tells us that, in this context, noble words about defending the freedom of the media are not only misguided but themselves offensive.

It is a curious fact that historically the development of attitudes to censorship has not been all one-way in this respect. The London theater of the Restoration period allowed a degree of sexual frankness and dissolute cynicism that could not be tolerated in the mid-eighteenth century, still less in the Victorian age. There were plays by Restoration dramatists which had to be bowdlerized for public presentation in the later ages. There were other plays that were kept locked away from the general public in library cupboards. We may well ask ourselves today what is the larger historic significance of the shift from Victorian restraint to contemporary frankness in this respect. When we consider what is allowed today in print, and on the stage and the screen, as opposed to what was permitted last century or indeed fifty years ago we recognize a historic revolution.

I have just read an article on the contemporary London theater in the weekly journal *The Spectator.* It is written by Harry Eyres and is headed "Sensation stalks the London stage."

At moments recently it has seemed that the theatrical powers-that-be, following the example of visual arts and cinema, have decided that audience's attention can only be held by acts of ever-grosser lewdness, pointless violence or self-destruction.

The critic then goes on to illustrate what he means by "acts of ever-grosser lewdness." The vocabulary used is perhaps best avoided in a book destined for the religious public. But it specifies acts of anal sex, of oral sex, of self-pleasuring and of straight coition. Such acts, he complains, are as common in the plays of three-named dramatists "as the taking of tea or pre-prandial drinks used to be in the theatre of T.S. Eliot and Noël Coward.... Acts whose public performance would occasion arrest have taken the place of arresting thought, language or imagery." Harry Eyres quotes a statement by Paul Valéry made seventy years ago. "When you cannot interest people in anything else, you expose only pudenda to the public view."

Casting our minds back to the ethos of the Victorian theater, how do we account for the historical phenomenon represented by so preposterous a change in taste from one age to another? It would be simplistic to explain this change merely in terms of increasing irreligion and the decline of Christianity. The Christianity of the Victorian age was socially pervasive, but much of it was a matter of respectability rather than of deeply felt conviction. Nevertheless, Christian influence spilled over into public life, exercising a powerful influence on public habits. Certainly it is fair to label the now-established resistance to constraints on what is said or seen in public or in print as a product of the post-Christian mind.

However, the popular post-Christian view that twentieth-century manners have released us from a negative Victorian prudery over sexual matters is questionable. Words like "prudish" and "puritanical" scarcely do justice to the Victorian attitude to sex. The size of Victorian families indicates an uninhibited level of sexual activity. It could be argued that the Victorians were much more conscious of the power of sex than we are. That could be why women were distanced from men by complex etiquettes of contact in social life. There was a time when female employees in certain respectable institutions were required to lower their eyes when conversing with male colleagues. The ethos behind this distancing must surely have been based on a recognition of the compulsive force of the sexual appetite. On those grounds the Victorians would never have been so rash as to put both sexes together in comparable stations, say, on a warship. We, who have seen what doing so has led to, may perhaps concede their prudence. The Victorians seem to have believed in the need to tame sexuality and domesticate it. We find in Victorian literature the image of the virginal young woman who seems chastely remote from contact with the earthiness of procreation. She is someone in whose presence animal appetite is chilled into awe. This image, the angel in the house, was surely not the product of male minds castrated by dwelling in the world of top hats that had to be decorously lifted at the sight of a skirt. It was the product of male minds alert to the bubbling cauldron of sexuality that seethed beneath the surface of interchange between the sexes.

Study the sentimental ballads by which romantic tenors enraptured the company in the drawing rooms of country mansions and city villas.

In the gloaming, oh my darling,
When the lights were dim and low,
Was it wrong for me to love you
As we did so long ago?

There is verbal restraint here, but the underlying emotive thrust is undeniable. And the blend of politeness and potency lingered on in popularity into the early twentieth century.

Macushla, Macushla, your red lips are saying
That death is a dream and that love is for ay.

By comparison with these tear-jerking idioms many of the often inane lyrics of today's pop scene, even the overtly sexual ones, are emasculated of emotion. The question raised implicitly is whether the post-Christian writer's and artist's external obsession with sex is perhaps the product of minds unequipped to grapple with the inner reality of its driving power. They do not plumb its emotional undercurrents. For they have lost the sense of its demonic dimensions and its potential for sublimity. There is no point in reining a dying horse.

When Bernard Shaw said that "assassination is the extreme form of censorship" he was making the point that censorship is a form of obstruction, and that the ultimate and final obstruction to any human activity is death. But clearly not every form of obstruction is negative in its purpose. Two motives for obstruction must be distinguished. I see an attractive pathway leading into woods at the side of a country road. It is a broad pathway and well-surfaced. There might be a delightful spot for a picnic in there. But I find that there is a locked gate to prevent anyone from going in. And there is a notice which says, "PRIVATE—Trespassers will be prosecuted." Why is this so? In whose interests is free use of this path obstructed? Are there dangerous beasts about in the wood? Was the ground mined in some military maneuver? No. Freedom of access is banned in order to protect Lord Brass' estate from invasion by city workers taking a day off in the countryside. I am naturally tempted to feel a bit resentful against Lord Brass and his kind.

But there are other kinds of obstruction on my freedom of movement. I have lately found an attractive road in our area which has been blocked off at the crossroads by which we should normally approach it. "ROAD CLOSED," a notice reads. Inquiring the reason for this, I am soon enlightened. The road sweeps downhill from the crossroads, bends sharply at the bottom to cross a narrow bridge, then bends sharply again to climb out of the valley. A truck driver misjudged the first bend, crashed through the wall and finished up in the river below. There was the danger that a motorist might follow through the gap in the wall that the truck driver had made. Complicated road works are afoot to restore the bridge. It is too narrow to be repaired and used at the same time. Freedom of movement is banned in order to protect motorists from danger and assist restoration of the route.

Lord Brass' obstruction of my freedom produces a different reaction in me from the obstruction by the local authority. Obstruction in the interests of the obstructor is a very different thing from obstruction in the interests of the obstructed. The act of obstruction requires an obstructor; in the cases I have cited that obstructor is Lord Brass or the local authority in control of the roads. It also requires what the medical men call an "obstruct"; in the cases I have cited that is a locked gate labeled "PRIVATE" and a barrier labeled "ROAD CLOSED." And in the third place the act of obstruction requires what I shall call an "obstructee"; that is you or me, prevented from going where we want to go.

Obstructees may have a highly developed sense of what is just and what is unjust, what is generous and what is mean, and they respond with corresponding emotions to the obstructions I have described. But if obstructees may, in some cases, feel righteous indignation when confronted by obstructions, are there not occasions when righteous indignation might be stirred by the lack of any obstruction? How should I have felt if I had driven down the road to the broken bridge not forewarned of the hazard ahead?

The form of obstructionism that constitutes "censorship" is complicated by the fact that there are two kinds of obstructee. There are the writers who are obstructed from saying what they want to say, and the readers or the audience who are obstructed from reading or hearing it. There are the artists who are prevented from representing what they want to represent, and the public who are prevented from seeing it. This gives the population at large an interest in the issue of censorship. If an opinion survey asked people whether they approved of any form of censorship, I suspect there would be a general thumbs-down for it. There is, as we have said, a general, vague feeling abroad that all censorship is a bad thing, for the post-Christian media have conveniently neglected to apply the word "censorship" where it belongs—for instance, to legislation against racially offensive propaganda.

One may misjudge the public mood in this respect. Not long ago I saw a contemporary play. It concerned a pattern of home life and family relationships clearly damaged by a skeleton in the closet. And equally clearly the skeleton was in the private closet of the husband and father around whom the household was built. The dramatist's technique was to keep the

audience guessing about what this householder and businessman was uncomfortably trying to hide from investigation. Was
he perhaps covering up on someone else's behalf? Was he guilty
of some terrible deed in the past? When the dénouement came
the dreadful truth emerged that this at first seemingly
respectable gentleman's prosperity was built on the seedy business of making pornographic videos.

I was interested in the fact that the dramatist could rely on
the powerful feelings of the audience in sheer disgust at this
activity. I asked myself whether the audience's shock would
have been greater or less if the householder had been revealed
as a burglar or a pimp. And I came to the conclusion that the
dramatist had quite correctly calculated on there being the
maximum shock value in the association with pornography.
And yet ... and yet ... Is there all that clear a line between the
sustained obscenities of the blue film and the sustained violence
of supposedly respectable films that people have been persuaded to treat as acceptable? We perhaps ought to worry more
about this. Already some of the most savage crimes of violence,
even those committed by youngsters, are being proved to be
imitative of what the offenders have seen on the TV. Perhaps
the post-Christian misuse of the concept "freedom" is seen at
its most damaging in the license it allows to the corruptors of
our young.

In the past, blasphemy and profanity as well as obscenity and
indecency were contained by censorhip. The post-Christian
mind has tolerated ventures into profanity which would have
shocked previous generations. The change is not just a matter
of what has happened in the field of entertainment and the arts.
It is not long ago that churches throughout the United

Kingdom could be left unlocked. It was common practice, while out walking or driving in rural areas, to pop into a village church and savor something of the history of the place by studying the memorial plaques and monuments. A prevailing feeling of respect for the sacred prevented people from going into churches to steal or vandalize objects inside. A certain awe of the house of God possessed people. In large areas of the country it is now no longer possible to leave the doors of churches unlocked. Insurance companies would not allow it. The caution that prevented criminals from including places of worship among their hunting grounds was no doubt in part a lingering superstition left over from less skeptical ages. It was part and parcel of the attitude that kept the shops and places of entertainment closed on Sundays.

The assumption that Sunday was "different" extended over the population quite outside the ranks of those for whom church attendance was a regular practice. Similarly, standards of taste drew the line at mention of God or Christ or matters spiritual in comedy shows. Among most people there was no great "Christian" consciousness at large behind these inhibitions. An unspoken etiquette emanated from seriously Christian circles and spread vaguely among the bulk of the population. Traces of constraints that had been firmly accepted in respectable Victorian households lingered into our own century. You might play Bach on the piano on a Sunday, but you would not play a cheap music-hall song. Families might gather together around the piano and sing hymns, but they would not play frivolous party games together. A child might begin to whistle a popular tune or to throw a ball about in the garden, and might thus provoke the mild parental rebuke, "Don't you know what day it is?"

One must repeat that there was often no specifically "Christian" consciousness behind these constraints. But their very existence and subsequent disappearance represent a challenge to us to make sense of current attitudes. We Christians encounter a similar challenge when we hear how Salman Rushdie's novel *The Satanic Verses* has provoked the imposition of a *fatwa* upon him by a government in the Muslim world. He has ridiculed the faith of Muslims and that in itself calls for the death penalty. We all find this barbaric. Yet we Christians are needled at the back of our minds by the thought, "How seriously these people take their religion and the dignity of their prophet!" And then we recall some offensive obscenity directed at the figure of Christ, and we are told that it is a work of art. I see in the press the picture of an album of items from the world of rock which is called "The Holy Bible" and the performers call themselves "Manic Street Preachers." An illustrative picture presents three obese (pregnant?) women holding their skirts above their hips. We are told that among the themes musically treated in the collection are self-mutilation, anorexia, serial killing and sexual consumerism. The curious wish to give this collection a bogusly sacred flavor is further evidence of the post-Christian attempt to expunge boundaries between category and category. This is central to the process of civilizational decomposition.

The post-Christian mind has operated to persuade the public that there are no boundaries of good taste or decency which cannot be crossed in the name of "art." There is plenty of evidence that the public can be bamboozled into acceptance of any profanity, absurdity or obscenity if self-assumed artistic authority so decrees. My newspaper today has an interesting item in this connection. It gives an account of an exhibition of young British artists' work at the National Museum in Wellington, New Zealand. Two exhibits have excited controversy. One is "a statue of the Virgin Mary encased in a condom," the work of Tania Kovats.

> Cheryll Sotheran, the museum chief executive, said that Ms. Kovats' piece reflected her desire to place a figure for which she had deep respect, the Madonna, in the context of her own life as a young woman in contemporary Britain.

There is a good deal more of the expected pretentious "artspeak" about raising issues of safe sex, abortion and so on. Another exhibit is "Sam Taylor-Woods' version of Leonardo da Vinci's *Last Supper*, with Jesus as a topless woman." There have been protests against these exhibits from Christians, to no avail of course, though a spokesman for the protesters has rightly pointed out that if a comparable exhibit had offended the Maoris, there would have been an instant reaction by the museum authorities. The prevalence of double standards in this respect is now evident in our countries.

It is one of the oddities of the situation that so many reasonably sensible people, who would quickly be persuaded to see through pretenses and deceptions in the political field, are only too ready to have the wool pulled over their eyes through their awe of self-proclaimed authorities in the artistic field. At supposedly high-brow exhibitions in London the artist Helen Chadwick's *Effluvia* included a mold of the shape made in snow by her own urine, and Damien Hirst suspended a dead sheep in a glass case in formaldehyde. Other delights include wallpaper made with a design of genitalia and, perhaps most astonishing of all, outstanding works by the Italian artist Piero Manzoni. These include his "living sculptures," works of art created by his trick of penning his own signature on the bodies of beautiful women. They also include his most celebrated effort, the cans of *Merda d'artista*, tins of his own excrement numbered for sale. The term "conceptual art" is utilized for this kind of experiment.

And now the latest news in the art world is that Damien Hirst, he of the dead sheep in formaldehyde, is working on a seven-foot "spot" painting, and he has allowed his two-year-old son a free hand in defacing it. Apparently this artwork is to join other works of the same kind to which the artists' children have been allowed to contribute. They are called "collaborations." A cynical critic of this kind of art has suggested that Damien Hirst could increase the value of the piece further if he were personally to vomit over it. Artists, of course, have often had need to reject established conventions and have thereby been fiercely attacked by their contemporaries. It is difficult for the layman to pass judgment on what may be new developments of technique, but where the very frameworks of a given medium are destroyed something more than an issue of aesthetic change is involved.

Not all the absurdities of the new "art" world involve profanity or obscenity. There was nothing either profane or obscene about suspending a dead sheep in formaldehyde. Some "creations" merely testify to a kind of infantile exhibitionism. We hear that a man is to stay boxed up inside a metal case for a week, in total darkness, with nothing but a supply of water and some machinery for getting rid of his waste. He will not be within hearing. Now, the man has a perfect right to behave thus. And no moral issue arises. But a question mark arises over the fact that it is done in a gallery and is represented as a work of "art." The proper place for such antics would be a circus.

What the post-Christian mind is about again is the obliteration of boundaries and categories. If what might be appropriately put on display in an art gallery is not to be differentiated from what might make a comic or half-comic side show at a circus, boundaries important to the survival of our culture have been removed. The word "music" can be applied to the symphonies of Beethoven, or to the cheapest and absurdest productions of rock or rap. Lovers of classical music may quite properly resent this, but no one can deny that a common medium is involved in the production of notes and a common skill required for performance on musical instruments. No such common relationships exist between the work of Michelangelo and the cans produced by Manzoni. What makes a great painting is one thing; what makes Manzoni's cans is another thing. The obliteration of such differentiae is crucial to the assault on Christianity and on civilization. Call the opposites by the same name. Celebrate divorce with a ceremony as well as marriage. Put cans of excrement on a level with the best that an artist can create. Tash is Aslan. Aslan is Tash.

A slightly different issue is involved in the excesses of photographers who have shocked public opinion. Here it is simply the choice of subject matter that is open to question. A camera is a piece of machinery and there is only one function it can serve. The American photographer Joel-Peter Witkin and the British photographer Robert Mapplethorpe have both come under fire from the authorities in this respect. Witkin has been accused of depravity and degeneracy for collecting corpses from morgues, then dismembering, dissecting and mutilating them for photographic use. In one composition a headless man is seated on a chair; in another, a head has been split in two so that the two halves can kiss each other; and in another, flowers sprout from a pateless skull. There is a mock-up of a Dutch still life which has severed human hands and feet scattered about.

We are told that Witkin's private life matches his work in its unorthodoxy. He has long lived with his wife and her female lover, sharing the same bed together. After interviewing him and learning about such matters, the journalist Alan Franks adds this curious piece of information: "He also talks, sometimes openly and sometimes coyly, about having sex with his subjects and about the profound Christianity which he insists informs his work." This surely gives us a prize instance of a mind consciously involved in the decomposition of categories and concepts. Accepted values and categories are scrapped. If you said of someone, "He prides himself on his career of successful thieving and on his profound Christianity," those who heard you might smell a rat. But in the world of art you can get away with that kind of nonsense.

Fifteen

Economic Freedom

W e have seen how in many areas the post-Christian mind is far too ready to accept without question features of contemporary life which really demand scrutiny. There is a natural tendency for growing human beings to accept as a norm the environment in which they are brought up. Some capacity for philosophical reflection is needed if one is to question things in the environment which everyone else seems to take for granted. The Christian faith has an educative influence in this respect. It requires us to survey our surroundings in the light of a supernatural reality which transcends the limited perspectives of a given century, indeed, of a given civilization. Immersion in the tradition of a faith that puts the world under judgment inevitably sharpens the mental antennae in responding to aspects of the contemporary scene that seem to be gravely corrupting or to be especially characterized by ephemerality or triviality.

We have looked critically at the abuses tolerated under shelter of the words "freedom of expression." One may doubt whether there are equally dangerous abuses sheltered by comparable expressions such as "political freedom" or "economic freedom." Nevertheless, the latter expression at least deserves Christian scrutiny. Political freedom gives people the right to choose their own governments and to be ruled justly without tyranny. Yet we recognize that, however thoroughly that freedom is granted and exercised, those who are so governed will not necessarily escape grave inequality. They may enjoy a system of representative government that satisfies every demand for freedom, and yet even so they may find themselves in a society riddled with inequalities, a society in which many people suffer poverty and privation while others abound in wealth and luxury.

Is it just to speak of the poor and the deprived as enjoying "economic freedom"? When we speak of "economic freedom" we generally refer to the right of people to indulge in agriculture and commerce, trade and industry, unhampered by state controls. The so-called free market is assumed to have the capacity to shed material benefits on the population at large. And yet, ironically enough, the more this freedom of the market is guaranteed, the more likely it seems to be that inequalities in material well-being will be intensified. If the total wealth of a nation is increased, it does not follow that the benefits will be fairly shared by all.

Idealistic attempts to reform economic systems in the interests of equality have never been very successful. We all know that if a capitalist system is operated by selfish, ungenerous people, it can produce misery and injustice. We know equally too that if a socialist system is in the hands of selfish, ungenerous people it will also produce misery and injustice. Christian awareness of the basic relevance of the moral law to every sphere of human activity tends to cut us off from meaningful discussion on levels of discourse that bypass this fundamental premise. We may become rationally convinced that a given political system is vastly superior to others, but we cannot forget that evil people can corrupt any system, perverting it to their own ends. Similarly good people can mitigate the ill effects of an inferior system.

This has to be said because there are those nowadays who seem to want to browbeat us into operating mentally on that level of discourse that bypasses the moral dimensions. They want to argue about political and economic theories as though they could be put into practice in areas of conduct hygienically insulated from truly human motivations. To focus on truly human considerations is to focus on living beings who daily choose between good and evil. That is what human beings are doing all the time, hourly deciding whether to be selfish or unselfish, whether to be greedy or considerate of others, whether to be honest or slightly dishonest or thoroughly dishonest. These potentials affect the operation not just of *some* spheres of human intercourse but of *all* spheres of human intercourse. Just as the choices made between these alternatives determine the character and quality of personal and domestic life, so too they determine the character and quality of commercial and industrial transactions, political and economic practices.

We cannot pretend that the use of the world's economic resources is a matter with no moral implications. I am writing on the day in which news has broken that India has carried out nuclear tests in the process of turning itself militarily into a nuclear power. The press is full of complaints that this has been achieved only by enormous expenditure in a country where the living standards of large numbers of the population, in terms of housing, sanitation, hygiene, education and other public services, would be quite unacceptable in the West. The question arises whether the economic freedom of individuals is jeopardized when compulsory taxation is employed to destructive ends of which contributing taxpayers would thoroughly disapprove if the implications were spelled out to them. It will be argued that in a democracy the will of the majority must prevail, and that in consequence there will be citizens paying taxes in support of many causes of which they disapprove. For instance, a State-funded health service may carry out abortions which a large number of taxpayers would believe to be immoral. Where decisions about such policies are democratically arrived at, they have to be accepted.

However, there is good reason to look at some of the costs imposed upon the public by private industry and to consider whether they do not constitute an infringement of individual liberty. There are rapidly developing industries in our modern societies which affect us all from day to day and whose operations raise certain general moral questions. These industries cleverly exploit mechanisms of the free market and, in doing so, have grown disproportionately in their influence upon human beings. I propose to take a closer look at two of these industries, advertising and insurance.

The advertising industry is one of those industries that has expanded enormously during the later decades of the twentieth century. It impinges on our lives whenever we pick up a newspaper or a journal, or whenever we turn on the TV. The curious relationship between the advertising industry and the public has always interested me. It seems to raise crucial ethical questions that the post-Christian mind is apparently happy to ignore. They are questions that surely ought to occur to any thoughtful person who reasons about the public features of contemporary life. Just occasionally they are publicly aired.

Some years ago I listened to a radio discussion about the cost of advertising cars. It was agreed between a commentator and a representative of the motor industry that the customer's pocket is the only source from which the cost of advertising can be defrayed. There was no attempt to suggest that advertising can in some magical way pay for itself by increasing sales. On the contrary, the speakers agreed that certain specified expensive models were priced in such a way that each customer paid $1,700 or $2550 extra for a new car in order to defray the cost of advertising. At a more modest level, for the run-of-the-mill car for the popular market, the sum of $119 was then cited as the individual customer's contribution to the cost of advertising a well-known model. Sometime later I read in the press an item headed "Advert blitz inflates price of new cars." The article presented the estimated advertising budget for certain car firms for the year 1994, and then broke the figures down to an estimated "cost per car." The cars in question were not expensive ones but designed for mass sale in the popular market. The advertising costs per car ranged between $163 and $782.

This system adds compulsorily to the cost of a car for the purchaser. And yet it is unrelated to the cost of the materials and labor involved in manufacturing it. In fact, it is therefore the equivalent of a tax. If this addition to the cost were imposed by a government, everyone would recognize it as a "tax." Now, taxation is justified by governments on the grounds that it helps to finance services required by the general public. What ultimately justifies taxation, morally speaking, is that those who pay the tax have the democratic right to turn against a government and vote it out of office if its taxes are considered excessive or improper.

What would make a tax improper? Presumably it would be improper if the resources raised by taxation were devoted to purchasing things that the taxpayers did not want or did not approve of. "Taxation without representation is tyranny" was the slogan of the American statesman James Otis, who in 1761 demanded liberty from oppressive taxation for the colonies. The slogan "No taxation without representation" surely represents a cornerstone of freedom.

My thesis here is that modern advertising has become an immense system of tyrannical taxation, for the firms that spend vast amounts on advertising distribute that money in ways over which the public who compulsorily contribute it have absolutely no control. Look at the glossy magazines sold along with newspapers or sold independently. Their colorful full-page advertisements for cars, food, household goods and clothes are plainly expensive to produce. And what is disturbing is that these journals could not be published were it not for the revenue drawn from advertisers. If I understand correctly what I have heard on the radio and what I have read in the press, then the last time I bought a car I myself contributed a handsome sum to the cost of sustaining this kind of journalism. Yet I find most of these journals unhealthy and objectionable in respect to the attitudes they encourage. They celebrate the achievements and careers of men and women quite unfit to serve as models for admiration. By shedding a false glamour over the sleazy worlds of addiction and excess, they minister to that decomposition of morals and standards which is corrupting our civilization.

And what about TV? This is not the place to argue whether the corrupting influence of TV outweighs the benefits it bestows in the way of intellectual understanding or cultural advancement. Yet a vast proportion of the programs produced are made possible only by resources obtained from advertisers. Have we thought out what this really means? It means that I cannot buy a bar of chocolate, a bar of soap, a tube of toothpaste or a can of coffee without making an enforced contribution to the maintenance of programs that I am convinced the world would be better without. Surely this is taxation without representation of a most tyrannous and reprehensible kind. Buying an electric shaver, stocking up with corn flakes, equipping myself with a new pair of shoes or a new printer for my work, I am forced into contributing my tax toward the upkeep of journals and TV stations whose productions I deplore and whose influence I find damaging. Who is going to come along and free the public from these iniquitous impositions? We have had government enthusiasm for allowing workers to opt out of compulsory contributions to trade unions. What about legislation to enable me to opt out of compulsorily contributing, day by day, to the demoralization of society by the media?

It might be said in reply that banks, insurance companies and the like subsidize opera and symphony concerts whose cultural value is not open to question. Well, I happen to enjoy operas and orchestral concerts. Nevertheless, I feel faintly affronted when I open my program, having paid for my seat, to be told that it is only by courtesy of an insurance company or a bank that I am there at all. These people are trying to humiliate me, I feel. They are patting me fondly on the head, telling me to have a good time with their blessing and urging me to think

172 / *The Post-Christian Mind*

more kindly of them hereafter. Yet I cannot but reflect that I have paid my share toward their patronage by the highly inflated house insurance premiums and bank charges imposed on me. Moreover, my neighbor, who can't endure classical music, has paid his share too.

Patronage by industry is presumably here to stay. When it is straightforward support of healthy sports, it seems unexceptionable. But when, as in the case of the tobacco industry, the support to healthy sports appears to be given in the hope of causing spectators to associate a dubious product with a healthy active life, then there seems to be an element of dishonesty at work. The basis on which the advertisers act is that the image of a product is enhanced by association. Ought a product to need that kind of enhancement? Ought it not to be valued only for its own intrinsic worth?

The question arises when I read that British Nuclear Fuels (BNFL) is donating thirty thousand pounds over three years to the Boy Scout movement. In return the letters "BNFL" will be incorporated on the scientist's badge awarded to those scouts who pass the appropriate test. A representative of the Friends of the Earth has protested against this strategy. BNFL is under heavy criticism from the environmentalists, and giving money to a good cause which is in need is a way of improving its public image. The Scout movement is again so richly associated with the freshness and vigor of youth, and with healthy outdoor life, that presumably the flavor of these qualities will wash off onto BNFL via the pretty badge. There is an element of cynicism here that too often marks industrial advertising in the post-Christian mental environment.

The advertisers are not the only manipulators in the contemporary world who impose a universal system of taxation. Consider the function of the insurance industry. As the decades of our century have rolled by, the cost of insuring a car or household contents against theft has escalated out of proportion to inflation in general. Why is this so? It is because thievery has increased. Our houses are much more likely to be broken into than they were in those blissful midcentury years when we scarcely needed to lock the door when leaving the house. Similarly the likelihood that someone will steal our car from a street or from a parking lot is far higher than it was a few decades ago.

To clear our heads on this matter we need to trace exactly the course of the money, the direction it takes between our payment of the annual premium to the insurance company and the company's payment of compensation to some householder whose family heirlooms have been stolen from his home, or some car owner whose car has disappeared from the parking lot outside his office. The course of the money does not really reach its end there. Neither the householder who has lost his heirlooms nor the car owner who has lost his car is financially any better off than they were before the thefts. The beneficiary of the insurance company's outlay is, of course, the thief. He is the one who started with nothing and finished with jewelry or a car worth quite a lot. What it all amounts to is that you and I and all other members of the public who pay our annual insurance premiums for our household property and our cars are contributing to a massive system of taxation whose function is to subsidize theft.

We hear of gangs of young people who plan and execute burglaries. They may well be on the job full-time. Since they are unemployed, they get the first part of their income from State benefits. These benefits derive from the government's official income from taxpayers in general. The thieves derive the second (and perhaps the larger) part of their income from the sale of the goods they have stolen. The goods can be treated as their own because the insurance company has purchased them from the real owners for them. We are surely justified in identifying the insurance industry as operating a taxation system for the upkeep of criminal classes.

By this system of insurance we have made it possible to put up with burglary. So far as our daily lives are concerned, theft has lost its cutting edge. In this way dishonesty ceases to be primarily a moral problem. We have turned it into a money problem, a matter of financial outlay that can be funded by taxation. This is just one instance of how basic moral dimensions are ironed out of life and forgotten. In a sense, we are all conniving with the decomposition of moral standards when we pay the premiums that make theft supportable.

Sixteen

Back-to-Nature Movements

A s the specifically Christian understanding of our world has been decomposed, a vacuum has been created at that level of consciousness at which people try to come to terms with the world they inhabit. Christians confront the trials of life and the spectacle of human failure with the sense that a great drama is being played out under divine oversight, and they believe that ultimately love and justice will prevail. But people deprived of such faith cast around for outlets for the frustrations and dis-satisfactions that experience of life stirs in them. In seeking scapegoats for human failures and miseries, some people nowa-days fasten on what seems to be the massive defacement of the created world by our technological civilization. During recent decades we have seen the growth of various movements un-happy with damaging aspects of that civilization. Many of these movements are inspired by reverence or at least respect for the natural world. Their adherents point out how insensitively we have treated the world of nature. We can see the evidence all around us in our industrialized landscapes. The post-Christian revulsion against the damage inflicted on the earth by advanc-ing technology is something with which Christians can sympa-thize. So too perhaps is the post-Christian suspicion of some of the developments in medical technology which seem to reduce the human body to the level of a piece of machinery.

The concerns of environmentalists and others who query various modern technologies extend widely. Certain "green" groups have been influential enough to have made an impact here and there in the political field. It would be impossible here to list all the numerous movements in question. They span a vast area of activity. There are those who campaign against the farming practices that are denuding our landscape sof hedges and reducing the bird population so much that some species are disappearing from our land. There is the lobby that campaigns against the use of chemicals and genetic engineering in food production. There are enthusiasts who are prepared to organize physically laborious resistance to the building of a new motorway or a new bypass through an area of natural beauty. And, of course, the pollution of the environment by the internal combustion engine is now recognized as a worldwide problem. In a very different area of experience there are the enthusiasts for alternative medicine, for homeopathic remedies, for soothing treatments like aromatherapy. There are some who make a more wholesale rejection of the patterns of modern urban life. Disillusioned with its artifices, they reject the "rat race" of city life and escape to the Scottish highlands or islands to live on the products of their crafts.

It is important here to issue a caveat. We must be wary of entertaining a false contrast between the natural and the civilized. It has to be recognized, for instance, that the rural scene which some United Kingdom enthusiasts defend so fiercely is not, strictly speaking, wholly "natural," but manufactured by human effort over the centuries. The fields, the hedges, the lanes, the barns, the farms and cottages which make such beautiful picture postcards are, as they stand, as much a product of civilization as the now defunct gasometer. That being said, most of us feel that it is healthy to set a high value on nature in the face of increasing urbanization of rural areas, and we sympathize with the aims of those who wish to preserve our beautiful and healthy countryside.

Taking a historic view, we can see that whereas nineteenth-century scientific and technological progress represented a massive movement toward the conquest of nature, the drift of popular thinking in the twentieth century has been toward a new respect, indeed a new veneration, for nature. The nineteenth century netted our countries with railway lines, and polluted our skies with smoke and our cities with dirt. The good side of the twentieth century's new respect for nature is evident in the movements for conservation of the environment. Recent international efforts to contain the emission of noxious gases that threaten our environment and our climate represent a case in point.

We need here to make a crucial distinction. To offset the natural against the urban and the mechanical is one thing. To offset the natural against the civilized and the structured is a very different thing. Nature supplies no tips for good conduct. To find one's deepest moments of fulfillment in contemplation of the world of nature is limiting to the human spirit. To worship nature is irrational because nature is natural, and human beings are endowed with ability to transcend and master the natural. All that has been achieved by the human race in the way of civilization has been achieved by mastery of nature, by building homes, building bridges, making roads, constructing ships, acquiring languages, establishing systems of law and order and so on.

We may justifiably feel that the process of mastering nature has in some ways gone too far. When we look at the waste and desolation left behind by the abandonment of outmoded industrial sites—coal mines, textile mills, gas works and the like—the heart feels that such despoliation of areas that were once idyllic rural environments must be unforgivable. But we cannot believe it was wrong to harness natural resources in the service of living men and women.

Perhaps at this point we need to add to our reflections the fact that nature not only produces what gives us our daily food and drink, it also produces what enslaves men and women to tobacco, alcohol, heroin and cocaine. Indeed it has been fancifully suggested that nature is in our age taking revenge on humanity for the spoliation she suffered through the effects of industrialization and urbanization. She is taking revenge by enslaving men and women to addictions. On this view the mastery of nature by humanity is now being revenged by nature's mastery over our addicted fellow creatures.

This needs to be said because not all "pro-nature" movements are healthy. For some decades the novelist D.H. Lawrence exercised an unhealthy influence on the young. His influence was probably at its height in the fifties and sixties when things began to go so desperately wrong. Lawrence was genuinely moved by the way the mining industry took possession of its workers, enslaving them to its machinery. For them, home and family could be nothing more than a "little sideshow." Unfortunately Lawrence's assault on the contemporary world too often put the natural into opposition to the civilized and even the intellectual. At the end of *The Rainbow* the heroine is left putting her hope in the rainbow. For nature's rainbow represents the world's "new architecture." "The older world is done for," Lawrence said of the book. "There must be a new world." And nature's architecture will symbolically supersede the archaic cathedral arch. Lawrence thus sought to detach the human being from the historical structures—social and moral—that constrained the passionate self with their cramping artifices and their inhibitions. He sensed the disturbing chasm between urban world and rural world, the industrial world and farming world, but his vision also contrasted the world of animal vitality with the world of culture. His recipe for renewal was to revitalize our humanity through our physical rootedness in the natural order.

Our attitude to nature may be distorted by misleading comparisons. The contrast between the beauty of a delightful rural scene and the ugliness of an industrial wasteland may be striking. But it would be unbalanced to pass judgment on civilization simply in terms of such contrasts. To compare the loveliness of a Scottish highland glen with the ugliness of a chemical works on Tees-side does not give a true account of the relationship between nature and civilization. Is more beauty to be found in the highland glen than in the streets of Venice or Florence? Civilization may destroy or enhance the beauty of our world. The chemical factory defaces the environment, but the Taj Mahal and St. Paul's Cathedral beautify it. Civilization turns what is wild and untamed into what is structured and manageable. It does so in the first place to render human life tolerable at the basic level of shelter, warmth, food and clothing. Physical structures are crucial. Houses are built, roads are made, bridges are constructed, harbors are designed. The purely natural environment is eventually patterned by networks of communication such as roads, canals, railways, telephone wires, electricity cables, gas pipes and sewage pipes.

The structured framework imposed on the external environment represents our outward mastery of nature. But it would be of small benefit to humanity were it not matched by mastery of our inner nature. Men and women live together usefully and harmoniously in society only if a comparable framework of controls is imposed on appetite and aggression, lust and greed, selfishness and hatred. Social groupings are established, laws are made. What roads and wires do to the physical environment, codes of conduct, judicial systems, etiquettes and protocols do to the natural desires, appetites and ambitions of human beings. They constitute a social fabric as needful to civilization as the physical fabric of house and road, water pipe and telephone.

Time and time again it has emerged in this book that we are losing the proper sense of our dependence on the structures that determine the quality of our civilization. The decay of the family is a case in point. The deconstruction of the family is taking place before our eyes. The replacement in the popular consciousness of codes to be observed by "rights" to be enjoyed is another such development. Comparable tendencies emerge in the advice to follow the feelings of the heart and not the dictates of the head. And although the issue ought not to be oversimplified, the same disastrous tendencies can be seen in the replacement of discipline and rigor in the classroom by techniques of "child-centered" education.

In many respects we have been bemused by what was in origin a healthy respect for the individual. We cannot condemn wholly the liberal determination that structures and formulations should not be allowed to fetter the individual. We have insisted, quite justly, on the value of the individual and the impropriety of shackling the individual by codes and regulations which seem to reduce one to the status of a unit in an aggregated mass. The Christian certainly has every reason to demand the highest rating for the individual over the pressures that reduce a person's significance to that of a cog in an industrial mechanism or a disembodied consumer in a nation's markets.

To add stature to the individual by downgrading demands made by the apparatus of production and consumption in which we are inevitably caught up is wholly justifiable. But it is absurd to try to add stature to the individual by downgrading the demands of the apparatus by which we are civilized—the demands of the law and the legislature, of the social and family structures that embrace us, of code and protocol and etiquette that smooth our relationships with our fellow beings. A man may be justly encouraged by being told that he is of infinitely more value than any number of shares that change hands on the stock exchange or of any world-renowned work of art that the auctioneer knocks down for millions of pounds. But to try to encourage human beings by implying that their individuality gives them a superiority to the codes and formulations by which civilization is sustained is madness. No human being should feel enslaved as a driver by the rules of the road. No human being must be encouraged to believe that their dignity as an individual guarantees them an escape from subservience to the rules of grammar or the rules of arithmetic.

This is not the place to try to evaluate the dozens of different movements, good and not so good, bad and not so bad, that have been spawned in the last fifty years under the post-Christian back-to-nature umbrella. Sometimes the Christian has to walk a mental tightrope when enthusiasts for this or that cause demand acquiescence in some seemingly worthwhile effort, half good, half bad, to counter drifts in our technological civilization. Personal rejection of our highly mechanized material civilization may be a Christian option, but rejection of the culture, moral, social and intellectual, which Christendom has bequeathed us, is not.

Seventeen

Charity and Compassion

The post-Christian mind prides itself on its compassion. Of all the currently fashionable virtues it is perhaps the most popularly cherished. Elections have been fought in the United Kingdom by parties in rivalry, each claiming to be more compassionate than the other. It has been felt necessary to make these claims because the public needed reassurance that the benefits of the national welfare services would remain commonly available to all who might need them. Promises of better funding for treatment of the sick and for alleviation of poverty are a necessary ingredient in political propaganda. If we pride ourselves nationally these days on one major achievement, it is that the public health service remains available to all without cost at the point of need. Only second to this in the minds of most voters is the demand for an assurance that if people fall into unemployment or poverty the cash benefits will be available to rescue them at least from the direst need. Since we Christians have always been taught that love, or charity, is the first of the virtues, surely we ought to find modern thinking in tune with our own in this respect. Up to a point we do indeed.

However, it could be argued that the readiness of citizens in the developed countries to organize health and welfare systems on a national scale is not primarily an expression of the general charitable wish to come to the rescue of all who are in need. Rather, it might be the expression of a general prudential canniness. That is to say, we calculate on the chances of being overtaken by personal ill health or other catastrophes, and we seek the cheapest mode of maximum insurance against such possible calamities. It is not charity that urges us to insure our house against fire, thus contributing our share to the accumulation of premiums that provide a rescue package for the unfortunate victim of mischance. The premium we pay is modest by comparison with the rescue package that will be available to any unfortunate claimant. We need to safeguard ourselves equally against the possibility of ill health or unemployment. We seek a comparatively painless way of guaranteeing that we shall be looked after if bad luck falls our way. The public welfare systems are national insurance systems for which the taxpayer contributes the premiums.

Recently right-wing thinkers have begun to argue that indiscriminately answering the needs of specified cases, such as single mothers, can cloud the judgment and discourage the practice of certain virtues. It is difficult to specify what is meant here without seeming priggishly judgmental. Sympathy is naturally and rightly called out for the single mother trying to do the best for her child on very limited means. Compassion is always aroused for those who have suffered at the hands of others. And the general assumption about a single mother in the past has always been that the father of the child has in some way or another let her down badly. If he had not, it was assumed, she would not be a single mother.

Our welfare systems were established at a time when the prevailing ethic thus limited the likely demands on them from single mothers. But under the psychological shelter of the post-Christian ethic a single mother may have three or four children all by different fathers. The example for this is set, as we have seen, by successful figures admired by the media. It is not reasonable to ignore the fact that women so placed are in no sense victims, but have actively chosen their lot. And indeed the situation arises where girls may choose to become single mothers without thought for the future needs of the child. In other words, our welfare systems have presupposed a moral climate that post-Christian thinking has destroyed. The financial implications of this revolution will eventually prove too costly to be borne.

Comparable problems arise in the running of the National Health Service. The compassionate business of providing free treatment for couples who for one reason or another are infertile seems on the surface fair enough. The techniques at present employed are expensive, but the founder and director of the world's first *in vitro* fertilization clinic has announced that new techniques will prove much cheaper. He was speaking on the twenty-first anniversary of the birth of the first test-tube baby. Among further new developments he foresaw was the use of a process for freezing ovular tissue so that, at a later date, eggs could be taken from it and fertilized. One particular application of this new technique would be to help women who have become sterile through cancer treatment. If the tissue is taken before chemotherapy, the woman's own egg could later be used to enable her to conceive. The motives behind developments of this kind are wholly charitable, wholly compassionate. Yet we cannot feel 100 percent comfortable with them. Do they not presuppose a humanity self-sufficient and independent of any higher order in the universe?

What makes this engineering of human procreation more questionable is that the same health service that supplies it is daily occupied in destroying fetuses for other women. The authorities responsible for various forms of artificial fertility treatment are also responsible for carrying out abortions day by day. One begins to sense some gross irrationality. This couple's ardent wish to have a baby is treated with compassion. That couple's ardent wish not to have a baby is treated with equal compassion. The net result is a health service that engineers artificial birth here and artificial death there. The Christian is bound to feel that men and women are trying to be God.

A comparable issue is raised by the provision of sex-change operations by the National Health Service. It is not possible for most of us to enter into the mind of someone who demands a change of sex. Consequently, one hesitates to make the urge the subject of argument. I suppose that Christians have always sensed that the finger of Divine Providence can be felt here and there in the course of life, especially in connection with the basic determinants of one's personal lot as son or daughter, as husband or wife, as father or mother. We cannot but feel that the post-Christian sense of total human autonomy somehow breaches the once-established provisos of human creatureliness.

If State-organized welfare systems that cater to the ill and the needy operate in such a way that sometimes people ask whether they are doing too much, independent charities daily make us wonder whether what we are doing for the world's poor and needy is not pitiably mean and inadequate. The organization of vast charitable appeals is now big business, and it touches us all from day to day. We can rarely go to collect the morning mail without picking up one or even two new charitable appeals.

One day *Help the Aged* urges me to "adopt a Granny" in some remote African village and save her from privation or death. The next day *Oxfam* asks me to imagine that I am a woman living in a village in the Sudan. One of my children died in my arms just after his second birthday, so weakened by hunger that he could not fight disease. My husband too has died prematurely. I am left with two small children totally dependent on me. The harvest is still a month away. My village ran out of food some time ago. All that remains is one cupful of millet per day to make a watery thin gruel. The daily dribble of thin gruel is never enough to satisfy the terrible cramps and cravings in my empty stomach. Having tried to picture myself in this horrendous situation, I am told that what the real subjects of such experiences need is twenty-five dollars from me. It will make all the difference. Alternatively, a slightly more modest sum would help a poor Indian woman called Bassawa to purchase a goat.

Of course, I recognize that these charities are employing experts in direct marketing to make the maximum impact on their mailing list. But I know too that they are not lying. They are not pure inventors. And if we are inclined to get so accustomed to these missives, indeed so overwhelmed by their frequency that we shrug our shoulders and stuff the appeals in the wastepaper basket, then conscience may disturb us uncomfortably.

Nor is the postman the only agent bringing news of human suffering into our homes. The newspaper, the radio and the TV all draw attention to the crying need for charity throughout the world. On one day we hear that fifty thousand people have lost their lives in an earthquake in Bangladesh. On another day we hear how thousands of Kurds are struggling to escape genocide in Iraq. Then there are the heart-rending accounts of famine in this or that part of the world threatening the lives of thousands. *Oxfam* asks me, "Did you know that every two days the same number of people are killed by starvation as died in Hiroshima?" And, as if that were not disturbing enough, I am told, "Every minute as you read this letter twenty-five children under five are dying because they don't have enough to eat...."

It is not only from the Third World that appeals crowd in upon us. I have a more local one before me from a daily newspaper. It is inserted there by the Motor Neurone Disease Association. "My wife and I used to enjoy an active sex life. Now I can't even move my lips to smile at her. I have Motor Neurone Disease, a fatal illness which gradually wastes away all your muscles, leaving you completely helpless. I can't move my arms, my legs or my face. I can't even speak. All I can do is lie and wait, and think about the life I used to enjoy." This appeal is a generalized one. Probably little can be done for the typical case represented. The need is for research.

Perhaps even more disturbing is a private appeal I received some time ago from a literary figure in Canada who was seeking help from fellow writers. At the age of forty-four, he was completely paralyzed and needed twenty-four-hour care. "I am imprisoned in a rigid body and cannot initiate any movement on my own. If I am not moved every few minutes my muscles go into painful spasms and I find it impossible to breathe." He was a victim of Parkinson's Disease. He was a candidate for adrenal-cell transplant surgery pioneered in Mexico City, but was judged unequal to the strain of cell-transplantation from his own body into his brain. He then became a candidate for a less taxing form of transplant, using cells from aborted fetuses instead of from the patient's own body. The treatment was being pioneered in Denver, Colorado. He was appealing for $30,000 to enable him to make the trip and pay for the treatment.

Laying aside scruples about the use of fetal material in such experimentation, we ponder the magnitude of the total cost—especially perhaps in relation to the slightness of the chance of real success. The question of due proportionality raises its head. We are tempted to ask ourselves horrible questions such as, "How many thousands of starving children could be rescued for the cost of this operation in Denver?"

Is proportionality a concept that Christians should ignore? Are we not taught that the ninety-nine sheep should be left to look after themselves while the lost one is laboriously searched for?

The question troubles us sometimes when we consider the current workings of the criminal code. The dreadful question comes to mind: How many starving children could be given a healthy diet, how many famished women could be supplied with goats for what it costs in our countries to keep in secure and bearable conditions the perpetrator of a string of murders? And it is not only in the case of murderers that such questions arise. A problem has arisen in the United Kingdom over the treatment of pedophiles. A dangerous one has served the due sentence for his crime, and compassion as well as justice insist that he be allowed his freedom. Sympathy for parents of young children demands that his identity should not be concealed, for parents are horrified at the thought that he might settle in their area. In consequence there is nowhere for him to live. So he is persuaded to accept voluntarily a place in a private clinic. There his upkeep costs the taxpayer something like $186,000 a year. That sum would rescue countless children from starvation in famine-stricken corners of the world.

The truth is that an odd kind of sympathy is stirred in us by the lot of the serial rapist or murderer condemned to life imprisonment. We say to ourselves, "Poor fellow, to have been endowed with such perverted capacities." From this thought follows another. "How appalling it must be to have to live with yourself the rest of a lifetime in the knowledge that you have caused such destruction and misery!" We ask ourselves, "Would you rather have been this murderer's victim, dead in your grave, or this murderer living with the memory of what he has done?" And we can scarcely think of a worse lot for ourselves than to be in that man's shoes.

Such a thought came to me this morning in a slightly different context. The news had come through by press and radio of the conclusion of a case against a driver addicted to alcohol. On a country road in Northumberland he almost ran over a man jogging along the side of the road. As the jogger was overtaken by the car, he noticed that the driver had a bottle of vodka in his hand which was held to his mouth. A few moments later the car crashed into the back of a group of cyclists riding in single file. Three of them were killed instantly. The driver was found to be heavily drunk. The deaths of the three men left seven children without a father. The news this morning was that the driver had been condemned to seven years in prison. It was said that he received his sentence in tears. "I should not have driven a car. I just wish I could put the clock back," he said. And small wonder, we say to ourselves.

The point I am making here is this. We feel we would far rather have been one of the cyclists; indeed, burdensome and agonizing as their lot must be, we would far rather be one of those tragically bereaved widows, than be in the position of this poor creature condemned to carry the guilt of those killings for the rest of his days. When we first reflect on the tragic events we see the widowed mothers and orphaned children as the lost sheep. But as the fate of their killer sinks in, he seems to be even more desperately lost.

The question of proportionality in official exercise of compassion arises also in dealing with those youngsters in our schools who are disruptive and resist proper discipline. A difficult practical problem arises here which modern civilization faces. How far can our educational systems tolerate disorder and interruption caused by a minority of troublemakers when it damages the progress of the majority of pupils? The irony is that, because the troublemakers are comparatively few in number, it is practicable to tolerate their behavior, but then the fact that so few disrupt the progress of so many creates an irrationally disproportionate use of resources.

We cannot touch on this topic without noting how the post-Christian mind's dislike of hierarchies discourages adults from exercising the degree of authority over children that once would have been generally accepted. In many areas of experience the readiness to break through old barriers of class and station is obviously admirable. I have just read how the Secretary of State for Health, in the course of surveying the current state of the National Health Service, has invited a hospital porter to join the committee that is inquiring into staff morale. This is surely a wholly admirable example of jumping over the boundaries between management and workers.

But in the same paper I have read another comparable item which raises questions. Panels have been set up by official bodies to inquire into the problem of truancy in schools. It is estimated that one in ten children misses some lessons by truancy during their school career. Habitual truants have been asked to appear before the committee to explain their reasons for their behavior. One girl of fifteen said she stayed at home to watch TV. "It's too much hassle to get up in the morning. It should start at 10:30." A boy of sixteen said, "I blame the teachers, because lessons are so boring and they have their favorites." Now it may be that the press is to blame for quoting these children—and for including photographs of two twelve-year-old girls who appeared before the panel, both looking consciously meditative and surly. But surely to give these wayward children attention and publicity to this extent is unhealthy for them and for others. The post-Christian mind has produced certain problems by its erosion of disciplinary structures which once firmly established the status of pupils in the educational system that catered to them.

It is fair to point out that many of the problems of criminality and of disruption in schools stem ultimately from the collapse of the Christian ethic of marriage and the family. One young girl quoted in the item on truancy to which I have just referred said quite frankly, "My dad does not know I play truant because he does not live with me." She added that he would "go mad" if he knew. This is a signpost pointing to the root of much evil. Time and time again we have had to return in this book to the issue of family breakdown. It would be absurd to apologize for the attention we have given to that issue. Behind theft and violence there is addiction, and behind addiction there is so often a history of family breakdown. Behind juvenile and adult criminality of all kinds there often lies the same root cause. It seems that we can scarcely overestimate the damage done by the breakup of the family, by easy divorce, by serial polygamy or by the increase in sexual irregularities. Equally responsible for such damage is that most devilish of all post-Christian developments, scorn of the codes and structures, moral and social, which have disciplined and sustained Western Christendom in the past.

Eighteen

Denigration of Christianity

The most direct exponents of post-Christian thinking are sometimes fiercely anti-Christian. That does not necessarily mean that they nail their anti-Christian colors to the mast whenever they touch on the subject. On the contrary, they have devised techniques of denigration less obvious and direct. A favorite technique is that of the oblique smear. This can be conveyed as a casual throwaway observation. The advantage of the casual throwaway observation lies in its peripheral quality. It is not a blatantly direct proposition that might openly call for a response of agreement or disagreement. It is rather a seemingly casually placed comment in the margin of the argument. The purpose of presenting it in so offhand a manner is that it will appear to be too obvious to require any elaboration or corroboration.

Examples of this technique are more likely to appear at the level of highbrow reviewing (or at least middlebrow) than at the popular level. In 1991 the American scholar Robert Bernard Martin published a new life of the poet Gerard Manley Hopkins, *Gerard Manley Hopkins: A Very Private Life* (Harper Collins). Hopkins was one of those young Oxford men who was inspired by the Victorian Anglo-Catholic movement and, like Newman, became a Roman Catholic. This distressed his well-to-do Anglican parents. Writing to Newman of how they had responded when he had written a letter to them to announce his conversion, he said, "Their replies are terrible." Becoming a Roman Catholic in England at that time could be costly in terms of public, social and career prospects. Hopkins was nothing if not thoroughgoing in his commitments, and he soon joined the Jesuits. His life, externally at least, became one of sustained obedience and discipline.

Hopkins' poetry was published only some thirty years after his death. It is part poetry of delight in God's world and his creatures, and it is part a record of the severe anguish sometimes involved in acceptance of his lot. Deepening the spiritual life under the rigorous rules of his order could not but be a strain for a man of such rich natural, physical and literary sensitivities as his. A searing intensity of sheer bleak bewilderment and torment emerges in what have been called his "terrible sonnets." In them he wrestles with the seeming stark contradiction between God's demand and the impulses of heart and sense. This disturbing record of the cost of vocation embraced constitutes one of the finest and most moving products of English poetry.

Martin's biographical study of Hopkins is not in itself what has sparked off my treatment of the subject here. Rather, it was a review of the book published in the United Kingdom daily, *The Independent,* on April 6, 1991. The review supplies an apt example of the fashionable denigratory technique.

It is not the purpose here to enter the controversy about whether it was a "mistake" for a man of Hopkins' temperament to subject himself to Jesuit discipline. We are told that the biographer, in the reviewer's words, thinks that the Jesuits, far from stifling his talent, "gave him a discipline he craved and needed." But the reviewer is not content to leave it at that. This is what she adds.

> One can't help regretting that Pater, who interested himself in Hopkins at one time, didn't convert him to pagan plea-sures; the procedures of the Jesuits seem infinitely more damaging.

The use of the powerful word "damaging" gives the reader a jolt. It is one of those terms that call for objective completion. Damaging to what? To health, physical or mental? To poetic productivity? That can scarcely be intended here since it has just been suggested that the poetic productivity might have benefitted from the Jesuit regimen.

So what did the Jesuit discipline "damage"? In what way were Hopkins' inclinations thwarted? There are hints through-out the review that Hopkins' inclinations were homosexual. He was "small and delicate almost to girlishness"; he wrote admiringly of "strong men endowed with the muscle" he lacked. So what were the "pagan pleasures" to which the reviewer regrets that he was not converted by Pater?* It might shed light on the reviewer's thinking if we consider the careers of one or two of the young writers who were indeed influenced by Pater's ideas and followed him in pursuit of "pagan plea-sures." For Pater was the arch-apostle of aestheticism. He emp-tied the high moral and artistic doctrines of John Ruskin and Matthew Arnold of their ethical content. For literary purposes

---

*Walter Pater (1839-94), Oxford don, essayist and fastidious prose styl-ist, was an enthusiast for the art of the Italian Renaissance but a total skeptic in religion.

he treated all religious experience as a mere adjunct of aesthetic self-nourishment. All Christian notions of vocation and self-offering are dissolved within the concept of the artist's perfecting of his own self-cultivation.

Thus those who may be accounted Pater's disciples include Oscar Wilde, whose indulgence in "pagan pleasures" led him to imprisonment in Reading Gaol and an early death. There was too a group of fin-de-siècle writers at the turn of the century who are generally considered to have inherited the mantle of Pater's aestheticism—Arthur Symons, Lionel Johnson, Ernest Dowson and others. Their lots combined produce a record of alcoholism, addiction, mental breakdown, insanity and consumption. I read of Dowson in a reference book that "his brief life, ended by poverty, drink, and consumption, was in tune with his aestheticism."

So were the procedures of the Jesuits "infinitely more damaging" to Hopkins than a life of hedonism, alcoholism and self-indulgence might have proved? The word "infinitely" suggests a vast disproportion between what addiction and dissipation did to harm the decadent disciples of Pater and what Jesuit discipline did to harm Hopkins. We are, of course, breaking a butterfly on a wheel. The reviewer meant to do nothing more than to smear the Jesuits, to insert a little propaganda which might subvert the innocent reader's values. It was just a case of hinting that sexual indulgence and other addictions are somehow less destructive of the human spirit than prayer and fasting, worship and discipline. In the process the distinction between virtue and vice is turned on its head.

The reader may wonder whether too much attention has been paid to a few words, perhaps thoughtlessly written, some time ago. It is partly because, by what seems a remarkable coincidence, I have more recently, in another United Kingdom daily newspaper, *The Times*, come across something surprisingly similar to the reviewer's particular comment on Christian disciplines. A distinguished biographer was writing about the life of Oscar Wilde after the completion of his prison sentence.

> His first days of freedom were gay enough. He spoke of Dante, and of his desire to spend six months with the Jesuits; this retreat would have been more unhealthy than a prison cell and, fortunately, his pious request was denied.

"Fortunately?" Anyone who has read of Wilde's last sad years of shabby decline into dissipation will wonder what the writer means. What fate could have been less fortunate? In what respects is the discipline of a Jesuit retreat "more unhealthy" than life in a prison cell? We who are acquainted with the workings of the post-Christian mind at the level of middlebrow reviewing will recognize one more contrived throwaway jibe at Christian practices.

The post-Christian mind will naturally be inclined to discredit Christianity. It is a weakness of human nature in general that we all like to feel that we are in the swim, up-to-date and not attached to old-fashioned notions. And it is perfectly easy to present what seems on the surface to be an objective survey of facts about Christianity in such a way that the writer invites the reader to share his own skepticism. The writer knowingly presumes upon the sympathy of the reader in what amounts to a devaluation of the Christian faith. An air of seeming objectivity in the survey of supposed facts conceals the destructive intent.

Such an attitude emerges in a recent piece written by Matthew Parris in an issue of *The Times*. It so happens that the British press is, just now as I write, taking note of the fact that the prime minister, Tony Blair, whose wife is a Roman Catholic, has been attending Roman Catholic services with his wife though he is not officially a Roman Catholic. Tony Blair is known to be a man of faith and a practicing Christian. Is he thinking of joining the Roman Catholic Church? There is a certain official public interest in this matter in that the Church of England is the established church and the prime minister is involved in the selection of its bishops. Might a practicing Roman Catholic be an unsuitable person to exercise this prerogative?

Now, it says something about public attitudes to the Church that no constitutional query has ever arisen in the past over the fact that agnostic prime ministers with little time for Christianity have fulfilled the proper official functions in the appointment of bishops. But now, with the hint in the air that the prime minister might turn Roman Catholic, the issue arises.

Matthew Parris has taken advantage of the current interest in this matter to write an article surveying past prime ministers and designed to prove that most of them were agnostic. This may well be so, but Parris argues his case with the support of generalizations which will not stand up to scrutiny. "Many British voters do not like politicians who believe," he tells us. So what? Many other British voters are overjoyed to be able to vote for a politician who believes. Then Mr. Blair, we are told, is going to church as an act of Christian witness, and Matthew Parris adds: "A Catholic idea, witness has been embraced by Protestants." This is a staggering error. When was "witness" not a cardinal duty of Protestants as well as of Catholics? Parris implies that the novel idea of "witness" was an invention of Catholics at a time when, far from being socially advantageous, to profess belief exposed a believer to harm. "This is just such an era," Parris adds.

Thus, as though he knew all about it, Parris goes on to tell us that the prime minister will have been encouraged by his advisers "to shut up." And so for a time, the journalist tells us without a shred of evidence, Mr. Blair will acquiesce. "He realizes his Christianity is a political embarrassment, but cleaves to it anyway." And now, the reader will observe, it is apparently no longer a question of specifically Roman Catholic belief that is at issue, but of Christian belief in general. It is a "political embarrassment." This is wishful thinking by the atheistic mind determined to make it seem that the tide is running against the Church more damagingly than it is.

After his introductory observations Parris settles down to a survey of the prime ministers of the last two centuries, asking of each whether he, or in one instance she, was a believer, an agnostic or an atheist. He is tolerably fair in most cases and, of course, the serious believers are in a minority. Chief among them, Gladstone, stands out last century as a man of deep and lasting Christian commitment. Twentieth-century prime ministers have not generally been in that mold. Nevertheless Parris commits himself to some questionable summaries. "Winston Churchill despised God. He had an abiding belief in Providence and Destiny, sometimes seeming to confuse both with himself."

Now this defamatory statement sounds very clever, but what does it mean? To despise someone is to take up an attitude to them. It is impossible to despise someone whose existence you do not accept. The devils believe and tremble, we are told. Then what or who are these figures "Providence" and "Destiny" in whom Churchill had an "abiding belief"? An "abiding belief" sounds like a strong and serious conviction. There appears to be a Churchillian Pantheon inhabited by God, Providence and Destiny. Of the three, we are told, Churchill despised the first and clung to the other two. Now in Christendom the word "Providence" is applied to God's beneficent and prescient oversight, and guidance exercised on the human scene. "Destiny," however, personified with a capital letter, is the agency that predetermines human affairs unalterably. It would be nonsensical to believe at one and the same time in a Divine Providence, which is essentially caring of human interests, and a Destiny, which is indifferent to them. Moreover, one wonders where the evidence is that Churchill postured or pictured himself in either role. The man seems to have known exactly who he was. In short, we are here faced with a lot of nonsense, and Churchill did not go in for nonsense.

False comparisons provide another weapon of denigration. If you put two items side by side as though they were closely comparable, the flavor associated with the one of them will rub off on the other. I have just heard an interesting specimen of this technique. It has been suggested that the extravagant public reaction to the death of Princess Diana gave evidence of an emotionalism that was not genuine but "fake." This suggestion brought the word "fake" into the public eye. So much so that a radio commentator questioned two speakers on the subject of the "fake." To explore the topic the commentator produced two examples of what might be called "faking" that have recently been publicized. The one example was that of an artist who practices and exhibits "active art." Her exhibition included a mattress in a room. The announcement was made that, in pursuing her enthusiasm for "active art," the artist intended to have sex on the mattress with customers who purchased her work. This announcement turned out to be nothing more than a publicity stunt. It was a "fake."

Now the radio commentator put alongside this instance of fakery questions about the Turin shroud, which is reputed to hold the impression of Christ's face. Devout Catholics are queuing up to see the shroud just now on one of the rare occasions when it is on show in Turin Cathedral. One does not have to be an enthusiast for relics such as the shroud to be offended at the juxtaposition of the artist's bogus offer of promiscuous sex and the ancient shroud which is said to bear the Savior's features. The lining up together of the two instances does its work. The flavor of cheap bogusness rubs off from the one on to the other. That, of course, was the intention behind the comparison made between the two.

We Christians are going to have to be more alert to the sly sniping at Christian belief which goes on in the media under cover of supposedly objective comment in the spheres of the arts and of public life generally.

Nineteen

Conclusion

We have seen the skeptical agenda at work in a number of different contexts. What emerges as we try to pull together the various strands of evidence gathered in our exploration of contemporary thinking? Recurring time after time are certain themes and tendencies. By reason of their negative nature, they scarcely lend themselves to systematic explication under neat headings. Nevertheless we recognize throughout that a persistent motivation inspires the sometimes disparate assaults on our faith. The motivation might lend itself to codification, if that is an appropriate term to define a series of processes of decomposition. The manifesto appropriate to those processes might be framed something like this:

DECALOGUE OF DECOMPOSITION

Where there are objective values, let them be subjectivized.

Where there are absolutes, let them be relativized.

Where there are intimations of transcendence, let them be dismissed.

Where there are structures, moral or social, let them be fragmented.

Where there are foundations, let them be destabilized.

Where there are traditions, let them be discredited.
Where there are distinctions, let them be whittled away.
Where there are boundaries, let them be abolished.
Where there are contrasts, let them be intermingled.
Where there are contradictions, let them be amalgamated.

It is not a heartening business to examine the climate of opinion that dominates popular thinking today. Increasingly we Christians inhabit an alien world. We cannot isolate ourselves from our human environment. We cannot turn ourselves into caricatures of priggishness who pass judgment at every point of the day on what our fellows are saying or what they are about. We learn to restrict open criticism to only the most offensive challenges to our faith. The daily, hourly evidences we encounter of the loss of Christian perspectives are allowed to float down the stream of experience unidentified and unchallenged.

After all, we are not usually facing directly answerable challenges to Christian belief and practice. We do not, for the most part, encounter a state of mind which represents Christianity as a formidable current foe or even which believes that it has discredited the Christian faith. Rather, we encounter a state of mind which has just left Christianity behind. We have been taught that the Church and the world must always be in conflict. Most of the time it is a conflict of mind with mind, but not in dialogue publicly articulated in speech or writing, still less in the challenge of outward act. This or that representation of the world we are up against—this advertisement or that TV show— touches our nerve with its implicit challenge to the Christian understanding of our human lot in time, but we shrug our shoulders. It is all we can do. Can one foresee, after all the years of our silence and seeming acquiescence in the making of a new paganism, the possible upsurge of long pent-up feeling, the possible explosion of long bottled-up frustration?

There is little evidence of that yet. But the possibility of an enlivened Christian responsiveness occurred to me when I read an item in a daily newspaper. It seems that the Italian fashion designer Georgio Armani planned an exhibition of his new creations in Paris. For this purpose a new marquee had been specially built over a fountain in the Place Saint Sulpice. Now the world of fashion designers, fashion writers and the celebrities who patronize them is plainly a world of absurd foppery and waste, about which we have had something to say earlier in this book. But it is not the kind of industry that stirs us to virulent criticism or active protest. After all, there are far worse human activities defacing our civilization than the parades on the catwalk. Nevertheless this particular presentation did raise a protest. Before the show could begin, a procession of monks, priests and religious supporters arrived to protest against the use of what they considered to be holy ground for this sacrilegious purpose. The religious objectors were supported by environmentalists who wanted the square preserved for the enjoyment of citizens. The determination that the show should not go ahead produced chaos and, in fact, the police had to cancel it.

Perhaps an even more interesting piece of evidence that a Christian backlash may yet be provoked by the current secularist drift into amorality is provided by a story from the United States. It concerns Tangier, a secluded little island in Chesapeake Bay, where apparently the inhabitants still speak a kind of Cornish dialect. According to my newspaper, Hollywood filmmakers decided that it would make the ideal location for certain scenes in a new film, *Message in a Bottle*. The town council inspected the script for the film and informed the filmmakers that they must either alter it or look elsewhere for a location. They found certain scenes involving sex and drinking unacceptable. There were also objections against the consistent improper use of the Lord's name. The council was unanimous in its decision. The mayor of Tangier, a descendant of the island's first settler, explained that the council was composed of Christians who could not put up with what was being proposed. Of course, there were some islanders who would stand to profit from the proposal and who therefore took a very different view, but one councillor at least has spoken approvingly of the publicity produced by the council's protest. "I think a lot of small-town America and religious groups would like to be able to see a movie that has been cleaned up for the moral-minded family."

Isolated instances of this kind can scarcely be regarded as straws in the wind, but they give encouragement to those of us who are anxious to clarify the immense gap now opening up between Christians and the culture of the world we live in. As I see it, the danger is that on the map of present-day presuppositional currencies, the Christian rationale will be squeezed into a corner. This will not happen because rampant atheism is widely articulated or consciously accepted in the surrounding regions. It will happen because a fog of furtive materialism reaches over the mental and linguistic terrain we all inhabit, and the clear light in which we can distinguish sense from nonsense is hidden.

Perhaps the imagery of clarity befogged smacks too much of a natural process and fails to reckon with the gravity of the damage that the post-Christian mind of the media is doing to Christendom. In the earlier decades of the nineteenth century John Keble prayed movingly for God's blessing on us: "Till in the ocean of thy love, We lose ourselves in heaven above." And, in the later decades of the century, reflecting a very different understanding and in a melancholy mood, Matthew Arnold surveyed the beach at Dover:

> The sea of faith
> Was once, too, at the full, and round earth's shore
> Lay like the folds of a bright girdle furled.
> But now I only hear
> Its melancholy, long, withdrawing roar,
> Retreating....

I do not believe myself that this accurately represents our problem today. The imagery again is too natural. The sea of faith is not retreating because the tide is going out. The sea of faith is being contaminated by the great oil slick of media innuendo, insult and misrepresentation. A vast campaign is needed to clean up the mess.